Digital Tools for Learning, Creating, & Thinking

Developmentally
Appropriate Strategies for
Early Childhood Educators

Victoria B. Fantozzi

National Association for the Education of Young Children
Washington, DC

National Association for the
Education of Young Children

1401 H Street NW, Suite 600
Washington, DC 20005
202-232-8777 • 800-424-2460
NAEYC.org

NAEYC Books

**Senior Director, Publishing
& Content Development**
Susan Friedman

Director, Books
Dana Battaglia

Senior Editor
Holly Bohart

Editor II
Rossella Procopio

Senior Creative Design Manager
Charity Coleman

Senior Creative Design Specialist
Gillian Frank

**Publishing Business
Operations Manager**
Francine Markowitz

Through its publications program, the National Association for the Education of Young Children (NAEYC) provides a forum for discussion of major issues and ideas in the early childhood field, with the hope of provoking thought and promoting professional growth. The views expressed or implied in this book are not necessarily those of the Association.

Permissions

NAEYC accepts requests for limited use of our copyrighted material. For permission to reprint, adapt, translate, or otherwise reuse and repurpose content from this publication, review our guidelines at NAEYC.org/resources/permissions.

Purchasers of *Digital Tools for Learning, Creating, and Thinking: Developmentally Appropriate Strategies for Early Childhood Educators* are permitted to photocopy pages 97–98 for educational or training purposes only. Photocopies may be made only from an original book.

Photo Credits

Copyright © Getty Images: 46 and 53

Courtesy of the author: 22, 39, 57, 72, 75, and 76

Library of Congress Control Number: 2021952718

ISBN: 978-1-952331-04-6

Item: 1159

Contents

Introduction

> It's a chilly day in January, and an unexpected snow has started outside the windows of Miss Michelle's pre-K classroom. The district announces a half-day, upending the schedule of the day. Four children sit on the carpet packing their backpacks and chatting:
>
> **ZhaoHong:** I have an iPad.
>
> **Leo:** My mommy has a black iPad and I know the iPad phone number. It's 7628.
>
> **ZhaoHong:** I know the iPad number and Mommy doesn't! (*Everyone laughs.*)
>
> **Ray:** Sometimes I ask my dad if I can have an iPad, but he just gives me his phone. I know that number and play all the games.
>
> **Carolina:** I have Netflix, me and my sister.

These children are talking about the technologies in their homes the same way they talk about their pets and toys. They compare their home experiences, perhaps stretch the truth a little, laugh together, and use conversations with friends to make sense of the world around them. Children are growing up with technologies as a part of their daily lives. They see adults in their communities using smartphones to text, read, watch videos, take pictures, post to social media, and, occasionally, talk. They communicate with friends and family via video calls. They watch media on TVs, phones, tablets, and laptops. They play games on tablets, smartphones, and video game consoles. They may or may not see any of the technology that permeates their personal worlds as an integral part of learning in their educational settings.

At the same time that children are experiencing and talking about technologies in their daily lives, families and the media are concerned about the effects of the omnipresence of technologies on society and especially on children. Families of young children grapple with whether or not to give their child their phone as a distraction when in line at the store. Concerned about their own and their children's technology use, some adults participate in digital detoxes and make rules about smartphones at the dinner table. Some discuss a "wait 'til 8th" policy to guide when their child will get their own smartphone. Headlines ask questions like "Have smartphones destroyed a generation?" (Twenge 2017).

Early childhood educators have begun to reflect on the role of technology in their settings and to pay attention to issues of access and equity. Some teachers feel comfortable making decisions about when and how to integrate technologies into their daily lessons; many do not. Some teachers worry that children will choose technology over the hands-on play with physical materials and interaction with peers that they know are so important. Others feel as if technology doesn't have anything new or valuable to offer in support of children's learning. Some teach in programs and communities with little access to or budget for technologies. Still others feel like it might be a good idea but don't consider themselves "tech savvy" and are not sure how to integrate technology into their teaching.

I worry about passivity around these topics: educators are often missing from the discussions in both families and early education settings about how and when children should use technologies. The integration of technologies in children's daily lives is only growing, and while families are making choices about technology use, it can sometimes seem as if teachers are forced into making choices about technologies rather than intentionally integrating their use into the curriculum. For example, some teachers are given devices or told that the school purchased an app or web-based resource, but there is little or no training or support for using the resources. In other settings, there is no budget for including new technologies, so teachers go without or attempt to acquire funding or devices on their own through charitable means, such as DonorsChoose.org. In the absence of active, intentional decision making by those who know young children and developmentally appropriate practice, developers of digital educational tools provide suggestions for technologies to be used in schools. In homes, game developers create digital games they describe as appropriate for young children, with a main goal actually being to make money off increasing time spent on digital applications (apps). Many of these apps, however, do not serve young children well. It is time for program leaders, school administrators, and teachers to take an active role in making decisions about what technologies to integrate into their educational programs and when and how. One goal for this book is to help educators to be more intentional in these decisions.

Guidance for Intentional Decision Making Around Technologies

NAEYC, the Fred Rogers Center, and the American Academy of Pediatrics support some media interactions for children over the age of 2 (AAP 2016; NAEYC & Fred Rogers Center 2011). These recommendations are grounded in the idea that interactions with technology are part of daily life and important for future skills in school and work. In addition, these organizations note that technology has advanced considerably from offering mainly passive interactions with TV; many new technologies are interactive, and some allow for open-ended exploration and creation.

However, "all screens are not created equal" (NAEYC & Fred Rogers Center 2011, 3). The Joan Ganz Cooney Center notes that the educational technology marketplace is difficult for families and teachers to navigate because of the constantly growing and changing offerings labeled "educational" without any expertise or research validating such claims (Guernsey et al., n.d). The lack of guidelines becomes even more problematic when it comes to apps aimed at young children. Many educational apps available in online stores are labeled with a broad age range, such as 0–5 (Sari, Takacs, & Bus 2019). Early childhood educators know that this age range is extremely broad; the development that takes place within a single year during this span, such as from age 3 to age 4, is vast, let alone the development that occurs from birth to age 5. Yet families have little to go on beyond an app developer's suggestions, top internet search hits, or recommendations from other families.

Further, although digital device ownership is becoming more common in the United States (Pew Research Center 2021) and globally (Silver 2019), many families still face challenges, such as lack of broadband internet or lack of experience with technologies. Informed teachers play an important role in helping to guide technology choices and model the use of devices and programs so that all children have experiences with technology that nurture them as active critical thinkers and participants in an increasingly digital society (Bales et al. 2020; Fantozzi, Johnson, & Scherfen 2018). It is critical that teachers build relationships with families that are respectful and reciprocal, not only sharing information with families but inviting them to be partners in their child's education through regular two-way communication and by collaborating on setting educational goals for their child and coordinating opportunities for families to share their knowledge and cultural assets with the group (Isik-Ercan 2020).

NAEYC and the Fred Rogers Center (2011) have called for teachers to apply their knowledge of developmentally appropriate practice (DAP) to support children and families in appropriate technology use inside and outside of school. Principle 9 of NAEYC's revised position statement on DAP explicitly states that "used responsibly and intentionally, technology and interactive media can be valuable tools for supporting children's development and learning" (NAEYC 2020, 13). But what does that look like? This book combines guidance from practical classroom experiences and the foundations of DAP to help education professionals consider ways to evaluate technologies, create a culture of appropriate technology use, and develop mindsets—both their own and children's—that are appropriate for participating in the ever-changing world of technologies.

Guiding Principles in this Book

Writing about technologies can feel like trying to cup water in your hands. Even as it's captured, the water spills out and is never contained entirely. Since the specific technologies available to teachers are constantly changing, making it challenging to talk about them, this book presents the following key principles to guide and ground the discussion about technologies and suggestions for educational practice:

> **Use of technologies in early childhood programs should be grounded in developmentally appropriate practice.** At the heart of DAP in any early childhood setting is the teacher as an informed decision maker. Teachers, then, should make decisions about using technologies with children, as they do with any teaching decision, based on three core considerations: what they know about commonalities in children's development and learning, the individuality of each child reflected in their unique characteristics and experiences, and the context in which learning and development occur, including the social and cultural contexts of the children and of the educators (NAEYC 2020).

> **Playful, child-centered environments are critical to learning.** Children should be empowered by their learning communities. Play allows children to explore and understand their world. In play, children build language, explore concepts, and develop social and emotional (Wohlwend 2011) and executive functioning skills (Diamond & Lee 2011). The uses of technologies explored in this book respect and support the learning gained through play. Play also centers children as creators and knowledge makers (Zosh et al. 2022). This book advocates for placing these technologies in children's hands so that they direct the learning and creating.

> **Technologies offer multimodal communication.** Many people think technologies in the classroom involve gamified learning—children pressing buttons to demonstrate knowledge and being rewarded by points, coins, or flashing lights. In contrast, this book advocates for using technology in a way that allows children to reflect on their work, tell stories, and express their creativity using pictures, voice, music, movement, and text.

An Explanation of Terms

Technologies: The *Oxford English Dictionary* (1989) defines *technology* as "the application of scientific knowledge for practical purposes," but the word is often used in the singular to describe a group of tools powered by computer chips. I use the plural term *technologies* to reflect the idea that technology is not one thing; there are many different kinds of technologies that can be used as tools to support digital learning.

Multimodal: A mode is a pathway for communication, such as a visual image, speaking, singing, or instrumental music. Teachers often use more than one mode to communicate an idea, such as mixing images, text, and their voices to teach a concept or using song and hand gestures to tell a story. Technologies, too, allow people to communicate in more than one mode, such as using images and voice or perhaps music and color, individually or in combination. This multimodal communication can enhance meaning and support young children's learning.

Culturally sustaining pedagogy (CSP): CSP is a teaching approach that builds on the framework of culturally responsive pedagogy (Ladson-Billings 2014; Paris & Alim 2014). Within this framework, teachers not only acknowledge and celebrate cultural differences but also consider the lived knowledge within the community an asset to be invited, explored, and sustained. Communities have shared knowledge in their language, communal stories, events, work, music, art, and traditions, labeled *community practices*; within a community, individuals may have similar knowledge and traditions related to their individual family's heritage or cultural background, labeled *heritage practices*. Culturally sustaining pedagogy aims to support children in becoming critical thinkers, reflecting on their role in society and their right to sustain their culture and heritage.

> **Families are integral members of the learning community.** Families are a child's first and longest-lasting teachers. They shape children's lives and should be welcomed and nurtured as partners in their children's educational programs (Mancilla & Blanco 2022). Technologies can also offer families a powerful window into their children's programs. DAP and culturally sustaining pedagogy approaches indicate that teachers should learn about individual families and their heritage practices as well as connect to the cultural contexts of the families' communities (Paris & Alim 2014). Communication should be bidirectional, with teachers sharing about the learning happening in the program and inviting families to bring in their knowledge of their child as an individual and share their community and heritage practices. This book offers strategies for building partnerships and connecting with families.

> **Everyone can use technology.** When teachers say they are or are not tech savvy, it implies that the ability to use technology is a gift that some people have and others do not. Although these teachers are referring to their own abilities, such beliefs and statements can "contribute to the inadvertent, often subtle or subconscious, transmission of low STEM expectations to the children they educate, especially to young girls, dual language learners, or children from households with low income or families with less education" (Chen 2021, 80). Technologies are tools, and using a tool is simply a skill. For any skill, some people will find beginning easier than others, some will have learned it from home experiences, and some will find that the way the skill is presented doesn't align with how they learn. People learn in varying ways and at different paces, but everyone can learn and be successful with any skill. Using technologies is no different. So, there is no such thing as tech savviness!

I hope these principles will serve as guideposts as you consider decisions about technologies.

What's in this Book?

This book shares a framework for thinking about developmentally appropriate technologies with young children that is based on current research as well as my work with early childhood educators. In particular, you will see references to four inspiring teachers: Christi and Anneliese, play-based preschool teachers; and Michelle and Debbie, teachers in a special education preschool center. All of these educators participated in intensive action research projects with me to explore how new technologies could support developmentally appropriate practices. Although these ideas started in preschool-based research, I (as well as other teachers and researchers) have applied them to pre-K through third grade.

I hope this book will encourage you on a journey of thinking about the ways you and the children you work with can use technology in developmentally appropriate ways. It is divided into two parts. In Part 1, Chapters 1 and 2 focus on big ideas to help you set a foundation: What types of technologies are best for the children I am working with? What kinds of thinking do I want them to do when they use technologies? Chapter 2 expands on these ideas to present a framework that will help you design ways to use technologies in your teaching.

Part 2 of the book focuses on practical steps for using technologies effectively:

> Chapter 3 discusses mindsets that will help foster a community that uses technologies creatively.

> Chapter 4 provides structures to help you get started teaching with technologies.

> Chapter 5 gives examples of projects using technologies that you might consider incorporating into your curriculum.

> Chapter 6 shares ways to use technologies to connect to families and invite them into your classroom community.

> Chapter 7 offers an opportunity to think about how an entire program or school community might commit to using technologies in developmentally appropriate ways.

What's Not in this Book

This book is not an expansive collection of every use of technologies to implement, nor is it a list of the "best" websites and apps. Technology is adaptable and changes at a fast pace, and there are far too many apps to list! Attempting to do this would make this book overly lengthy and quickly out of date. Rather, I provide a framework for approaching technologies with the children you teach. I will discuss how to develop a purpose for technologies in the classroom and criteria for technologies that support DAP. Technologies are here to stay, and this book aims to empower teachers to reclaim screens and use them for developmentally appropriate teaching.

PART 1

Setting a Foundation for Technologies in the Classroom

CHAPTER 1

Making Intentional Choices About Technologies

One morning, my 8-year-old son asks to play with the tablet. It's a snow day and he has been clamoring to go sledding and play in the snow all morning, but it's still dark, so I agree that he can play on the tablet while we wait for a more appropriate time to venture out into the snow.

When I later go to talk to him about his plans for the day, which will not include unlimited screen time, I am surprised to find him squatting over an elaborate LEGO scene taking a picture. He is in the middle of making a trailer using video-editing software. The week before, his class had learned how to use such software trailer templates to present information about endangered animals they were researching. Now he is using these newfound skills to create a trailer for an original story that can fit into the *Star Wars* universe. Working quietly in his room, he is positioning his *Star Wars* LEGO figures in a series of scenes to tell a story about three bounty hunters on the trail of an infamous criminal. He looks through a selection of video storyboard templates in the app and selects one with music that builds to a dramatic crescendo. He then adds the images of the LEGO scenes and a few lines of text that mimic language he's heard in movie trailers into the template, and in a short time he has created a trailer worthy of a summer blockbuster (directed by an 8-year-old).

He wants to share this trailer with friends, so we post it to Facebook where he receives a lot of positive feedback from family and friends who are amazed at what a child so young can do. Perhaps they shouldn't be, for just a short while later, he teams up with his 5-year-old brother and me as the camera operator to shoot a live-action trailer for a spy movie called *Agent Snorlax*.

Since these experiences, making movie trailers is something my children often do with their friends. Each experience illustrates how technologies can support playful collaborative storytelling where children mix their own ideas with popular culture and are able to share these stories with others. It's a wonderful example of who children are.

It is also a good example of who they are *not*. It's true that mobile technology has become a part of the daily life of young children in developed nations across the globe (Cristia & Siedl 2015; Rideout 2017; Staker et al. 2018). From infancy, they see people all around them tapping, swiping, pinching, and typing to take in or communicate information; thus, from early on, many children have an understanding of and take for granted how a touchscreen works (Harrison & McTavish 2018). In 2001, Prensky coined the term *digital native* to refer to young children who are immersed in a digital world and feel comfortable with a culture that uses technology for multiple means. What can be wrongly assumed about digital natives is that they have a preternatural understanding of technology and how to use it. Just because children may feel comfortable with technology as a tool does not mean that they will be independent with it without any instruction or scaffolding. In the same way that children gain emergent knowledge of reading from interactive reading experiences, watching others read and write, and receiving instruction, young children today learn emergent digital literacy skills by watching and using technologies with others (Marsh et al. 2017). My son didn't figure out how to make a movie trailer all on his own; he learned how to use this tool at school and then used it to create his own story. When he and his brother wanted to do a live-action movie, they asked me to film it and also to help them puzzle through the best shots to tell their story. Neither my son nor any of the children I work with possess special ingrained knowledge of technology. They do approach technology with comfort and curiosity, which can contrast with the discomfort that some adults feel about using technology. But it is important to remember that all of today's learners—no matter their experience with technology in their homes and daily lives—need teachers. Some children will learn to utilize technology on their own, just as some children learn to read without a teacher. But just as most children do not learn to read on their own, most also will not learn to effectively use technology without teachers to guide them.

Technology Is Not the Teacher

In the 1950s, behavioral psychologist B.F. Skinner proposed a teaching machine to revolutionize education (Watters 2015). This box would give a child one-on-one feedback based on work completed; a child would move on to the next assignment if they gave the correct answer but would repeat the assignment if they gave an incorrect answer. In this way, Skinner believed, they would learn incrementally and efficiently. Children could sit in front of this box daily, with little interaction with their peers or the teacher. These machines were, in fact, created and used in a few settings, but they never became popular (Watters 2015). The image of a roomful of children, each sitting in front of a box and mechanically moving through solitary lessons, is not one that aligns with developmentally appropriate practice (DAP) nor with an understanding of child development. Children need to be able to explore the world around them, use tactile experiences to gain new understandings, and work with peers and adults to gain social skills and construct new ideas. Yet research shows that when teachers do use technologies with children, they often treat the devices like teaching machines.

In many early learning settings and schools, children use technologies to work independently on a particular app that gamifies skills (Blackwell 2013; Lu et al. 2017; Mertala 2017). These programs require children to perform specific skills (e.g., identifying the correct beginning letter of an object or the correct numeral that identifies the number of objects), and they provide immediate feedback on performance in the form of points, flashing lights, or celebratory sounds. A child progresses in levels, and the skills get harder if the child is doing well; if not, they must repeat the level until the skill is completed correctly. While these games are used sparingly in classrooms, as opposed to Skinner's grander vision for learning with machines, the general approach to learning is the same.

In the context of DAP, these kinds of games do offer the opportunity for children to work at a level that is appropriate for each individual child—different children can work on different skills or skill levels. This shows some alignment with DAP by taking into consideration varying levels of readiness for each child and a point under principle 9 in the DAP position statement, "providing adaptive scaffolds to help each child progress in skills development at their own pace" (NAEYC 2020, 13). This feature can also make the games attractive to teachers because the apps tailor instruction for each child quickly and efficiently. However, the body of research about child development and learning does not support the idea that skill practice in this form nurtures brain development and leads to effective learning for children (Falk 2009; NASEM 2018). Principle 5 in the DAP position statement emphasizes the important roles that interaction with peers and adults, rich language use, and active exploration of children's environments play in children's learning (NAEYC 2020). Further, while skills practice can be a necessary part of a child's learning, using technologies does not offer the same opportunities for simultaneous small or large motor development as hands-on experiences do (NAEYC 2020). Finally, this use of technologies does not help prepare children to participate in a society where technologies are used to create new things, communicate ideas and stories, and collaborate with other people (Lynch & Redpath 2014). This use does not unlock the potential of the tools that teachers have available to them.

Most early childhood programs do not draw heavily from Skinner's approach to learning. Rather, many common practices are based on Jean Piaget's and Lev Vygotsky's ideas about how children learn about the world around them through exploration of materials and interactions with peers and adults (Mooney 2013). Although many teachers may not be able to name these two theorists, their work on early learning has impacted early childhood practice (Van Oers & Duijkers 2013). Both scholars emphasized the work and learning children do in play. Piaget suggested that children construct understandings of the world around them through exploring and observing. He theorized that children are in a continual cycle of taking in information, comparing it to concepts or *schemas* that they are already familiar with, and either *assimilating* (fitting in) new information to schemas they already have or constructing new schemas. This kind of learning comes through experiences with the real world. For example, when 3-year-old Miles plays at the water table, he comes in with some knowledge of water: it's in baths, he can drink it, adults use it to wash dishes, and it can get sudsy. At the water table he can take in new knowledge about how water flows, how heavy it is when it fills a bucket, and how it splashes from different heights. Vygotsky suggested that the interactions children have with peers and with adults, including the language exchanged in play, is essential to learning. At that same water table, and with a teacher's supportive conversation, Miles can begin to develop his understanding of new concepts such as *dripping*, *waterfall*, and *cascade*. Vygotsky also valued the dramatic play and story creation that takes place during play and the safe space such play offers children to explore new ideas and make sense of their world. Many early childhood educators know that important learning takes place through play, and yet when they use technologies with children, they use them more in line with Skinner's teaching box than with the way young children learn best (Mertala 2017).

Digital Tools for Learning, Creating, and Thinking

It is true that apps that provide skills practice through a game can support some opportunities for collaboration and exploration; it is possible for children to watch their peers play a game and learn some new vocabulary. However, many games do not allow for free exploration or discussion and can sometimes lead to misunderstandings or missed opportunities for learning. Three-year-old Amaya, for example, interacted with a game that was intended to teach beginning sound identification. She could control an alien dancing on a planet to catch objects falling from the sky that started with the same letters. This game was probably too challenging because her ability to isolate and match the beginning sounds of words was still developing, but she liked the little alien, so she played and played for quite a while without frustration. She did not play because she was learning letters; she figured out how to hack the game. In the game, the player is supposed to touch the pictures that have the same beginning sound. If the match is correct, the alien blasts off to the next letter, and if the match is wrong, the alien taps his foot. Amaya was happy with either response, so she contentedly tapped at the objects falling from the sky at random and watched the alien's response. The game was not teaching Amaya anything other than that if she touched enough items in the game, the alien would go in a rocket ship. Such games often teach unintentional lessons to a determined child.

Navigating Concerns About Technologies

Programmers who create these games are also at the center of controversy around technologies. In 2016, Tristan Harris, a former Google employee, referred to his smartphone as "a slot machine in his pocket" (Bosker 2016). He was raising awareness about persuasion design, or the ways that some app developers use knowledge of behavioral psychology to create apps designed to effectively stimulate the reward systems in our brains to encourage more time spent on the app.

Behavioral psychology looks at the way stimuli affect all of our behaviors. A stimulus is anything in our environment that elicits a response. If this stimulus is pleasurable to the brain, it is called a *reward*. In a game on a computer or tablet, a reward can be words or a sound when a level is completed. A schedule with an unpredictable release of the reward, in which an action produces a reward on a varied schedule rather than always following an action, is called a *variable reward schedule*. Researchers have found a varied reward schedule to be the most addicting (Sapolsky 2011). Much like gambling, where the next pull of the slot machine might get a player the win they crave, opening Instagram might give us a little endorphin hit when we see that someone has liked our post, so we check the app repeatedly and compulsively. Likewise, some app developers use this tendency to their advantage: some games, educational or not, use a system of variable rewards to encourage the user to play longer. The user might feel agitated when they must quit or bored when that steady flow of stimuli is removed (Steiner-Adair & Barker 2013).

Maryanne Wolf, a neuroscientist who researches reading and the brain, is concerned that reading via a screen may affect the way people read (2018). A print book, such as one being read by a parent to a child, is only one stimulus, allowing the readers to focus on the text alone. The reader can follow the story intently, consider multiple meanings in the story, and make connections to their experiences or to other texts, all of which are markers of deep comprehension. Wolf argues that screen reading is different because after frequent use, the brain learns that the screen can offer an endless supply of new stimuli (consider the last time you found yourself clicking a link or opening an app as if on autopilot). The brain can't completely focus on the text because the lure of new stimuli is ever present, so reading can become more surface level, reducing comprehension. Our brains are predisposed to prefer new stimuli; smartphones, laptops, tablets, and game systems are wired to provide a steady flow of novel stimuli. Interacting on the screen also allows hopping from one source of information to the next, attending to each new stimulus that pops up. This can lead to decreased attention even off the screen as our brains get used to hopping from one stimulus to the next rather than immersing deeply in reading (Levitin 2014).

It's important to note, however, that our brains do not respond to all forms of technology in the same way (Wolf 2018). Although professionals often use the broad label *screen time* for any interaction with a device, there is a broad range of potential interactions, and thus potential effects on the brain, with digital devices (Pappas 2020). Consider how having a video call may feel different from playing a game-based app. In an open-ended video call, the brain responds to social cues, and the interaction is likely more open ended and creative. A game-based app, in contrast, is a closed system where certain reactions receive rewards and the brain is rewarded with more stimulus if it responds quickly, leading to agitation. With many young children spending hours of their day interacting with a screen, it is important to consider the kinds of media interaction they are having and what this might mean for their developing brains.

Wolf, then, argues that rather than eschew all technology use, families and educators must make intentional choices about the use of technologies, especially with young children:

> I am convinced that with more wisdom than we have demonstrated to date, we can combine science with technology in ways that will help discern what is best and when . . . with all the mediums, devices, and digital tools at our disposal used optimally. . . . The reality is that we cannot and should not go back; nor should we move ahead thoughtlessly. (Wolf 2018, 126)

Recognizing that technologies are embedded in our daily social, work, and school lives, education associations such as NAEYC, as well as government and industry agencies, advocate for educating young children to utilize technologies. In fact, Straker and colleagues (2018) argue that

> Adults responsible for young children have an ethical responsibility to prepare them for life in a digital world. Assisting children to develop an understanding of the benefits and risks of digital technology alongside appropriate ways of using digital technology is an adult responsibility. (300)

Yet for the most part, families and educators have not been given good guidelines for making choices about technologies (Straker et al. 2018). Early on, the established measure for technology was screen time, which measures the amount of time that a child spends with a device but does not differentiate the type of media or interaction a child has with the media. Screen time as a measure, and recommendations associated with it, was designed to counter concerns that too much interaction with technologies would promote a sedentary lifestyle and the developmental and health risks that accompany it. In addition, the concept of screen time was largely based on research on television watching and has not evolved to reflect more interactive media.

Although screen time recommendations are periodically revisited and revised (in 2016, for example, the American Academy of Pediatrics updated guidelines to allow for video chatting even with very young children [AAP 2016]), Straker and colleagues (2018) argue that screen time recommendations do not adequately support families' and educators' efforts to make more nuanced decisions about technologies. If we accept that we should shape children's use of technologies rather than ignore, limit, or prohibit it, what guidelines should teachers use to choose technologies? Educators need to look beyond time on a screen or a blanket label of technologies as bad for children and consider how technologies are used and what purposes they can serve. The next section discusses both of these factors.

Close- and Open-Ended Apps

Mitchel Resnick, MIT professor of learning research, director of the Lifelong Kindergarten research group in the MIT Media Lab, and creator of the Scratch coding program, notes:

> **The focus shouldn't be on which technologies children are using, but rather what children are doing with them. Some uses of [technologies] foster creative thinking; others restrict it. . . . Parents and teachers should be searching for activities that will engage children in creative thinking and creative expression. (Resnick 2017, 25)**

Technologies can support creative, exploratory, and collaborative learning. Look beyond the device (laptop, tablet, or smartphone) and start thinking about what the children are doing with the device. This is an important distinction in how teachers think about technologies. Technologies tend to get labeled as good or bad. Yet technologies are tools that can be used in myriad ways, some of which are productive and supportive and others of which are not useful or are even worrisome. Rather than approach technologies as essentially good or bad, teachers must consider the kinds of technologies and how they can be used effectively in teaching.

Lynch and Redpath (2014) label apps in a way that can be helpful in evaluating your existing technologies and for selecting new ones. They label apps either *closed* or *open*; in this book I use the terms *close-ended* and *open-ended*.

Close-ended apps

> Provide gamified skill practice

> Limit children to working within a closed set of rules; they cannot create anything within the game or collaborate with peers or share their ideas with others within the game

> Use a system of stimulus and response; a user gets rewards for correct play or answers and negative feedback for incorrect play or answers

> Are generally used individually but can be competitive in game play or comparing high scores

One important question to ask about technology use is this: what is this tool offering that either helps children learn in a way that they might not be able to otherwise or helps children learn to participate in a culture that often uses technologies to communicate? Close-ended apps are not used to communicate, so we must ask if the application is providing some sort of enhanced learning. Sometimes these apps offer differentiated practice—for example, assigning children to varying levels of skill practice based on an initial assessment or immediately providing the next level of skill practice when a child quickly completes an activity. They can also be motivating to some children who dislike skill practice. However, as mentioned earlier, sometimes children can be too focused on trying to earn the reward, to the detriment of their learning. In addition, children often use close-ended apps to practice a skill that could be learned with manipulatives. For example, in the app Bugs and Numbers, children practice counting and develop number sense by moving bugs into containers. However, if this activity is done with manipulatives, a child can work not only on developing number sense but also on fine motor skills as they use a pincer grip to pick up small objects and place them in a container. When compared to counting with manipulatives, Bugs and Numbers may not be the most well-rounded approach to this kind of learning nor the best use of technologies.

In contrast, *open-ended* apps

> Present technologies as tools for making and sharing

> Support children in creating, whether it be by drawing, taking pictures, recording audio, moving characters, or a combination of these actions

> Have open-ended possibilities for use; the child, not the app, directs the purpose of the play within the app

> Allow for individual or collaborative use that is cooperative rather than competitive

> Generally have the capability to connect to other apps (e.g., photos can be uploaded from a camera to use in a digital book creation; a video can be shared to a class digital portfolio such as Seesaw or Tadpoles)

The goal with open-ended apps is not to individualize instruction but to offer children opportunities for creating, storytelling, and communicating, sometimes while working collaboratively. In addition, because open-ended apps allow for creation, the reward is internal rather than external, and children are less likely to experience agitation when their time with the app is done (Steiner-Adair & Barker 2013). Researchers have found that children are proud of the work they create with open-ended apps (Fantozzi, Johnson, & Scherfen 2018; Lynch & Redpath 2014; Petersen 2015).

Open-ended apps also can connect to other apps to pull information in or share with other sources. The camera app that comes with most tablets and smartphones is perhaps the most open-ended app. It allows for creating still images or videos (including time-lapse and slow-motion) that can then be edited and shared within the app or connected to many other applications to share or extend meaning by adding text, color, images, or music. When we consider what open-ended apps offer that close-ended apps cannot, we find that open-ended apps allow for mixing media, adding audio, reflecting on and reviewing work, and collaborating with friends. They can be used to create projects based on an assignment given by the teacher or to explore and create something completely new. Further, when children choose images or decide which text, audio, or music to add, they are learning multimodal communication, which is an increasingly important skill in the digital age.

Open-ended apps allow children to connect, create, collaborate, and communicate. Table 1 on the following page lists some features of just a few of the apps available as of the writing of this book, both open and close ended. The intention of this list is not to endorse or condemn these apps but to provide a framework for what an open- or close-ended app looks like so that teachers can make informed decisions about the apps they come across. Since apps change all the time, it is more important to consider the features of a particular app and whether or not those fit the needs of the children you work with. In addition, cost may be a consideration for a teacher or for a program. Many, but not all, educational apps are available for free or for free without certain features. Before you purchase an app, read reviews of it—these can be listed in an app store, but you may also find reviews posted on YouTube or from organizations such as Common Sense Media. The resources list on page 103 also provides links to a list of educational resources and communities focused on educational technologies that can support you in your search for apps.

Using Technologies with Purpose

Think about the apps that children are using as well as how you use the technologies available. For example, interactive whiteboards, or Smart Boards, are becoming more common in early childhood programs and are an example of an open-ended technology with many possibilities for creating and collaborating. These whiteboards connect to a computer and can allow multiple children to write or draw at the same time, offer shared viewing, and more. However, whiteboards are not always used to their full potential. Rather than transform teaching practices, the whiteboards are often used in place of an analog technology—for example, playing music for dancing on the whiteboard instead of on a stereo or writing with a digital marker instead of with pen and paper. Technologies' presence or use does not guarantee any form of learning; rather, the purposes that teachers set and the appropriate technologies they choose allow for learning.

An important tenet of DAP is that the teacher is an informed decision maker. Teachers must evaluate technologies critically by learning about them and putting them to their best uses. Chapter 2 presents a framework for evaluating technologies—both the capabilities of a given app and the ways teachers put technologies to use in their programs. At the end of Chapter 2 and each chapter that follows is a section called "Making Intentional Choices." These sections will highlight important aspects of using technologies and provide guidance for making choices about technologies in your program.

Table 1. Features of Select Open-Ended and Close-Ended Apps

Open Ended	Features	Accessible Devices
Shadow Puppet Edu	Allows for open-ended creation with images, including adding to the photo by drawing, typing, and recording audio Connects to databases of images (for example, a NASA database) as well as to the camera roll on the device so that children can select a photo from a database or take a photo for use in their project Easy to use for an individual child or an entire class	Smartphone, tablet
Toontastic	Allows children to create virtual puppet shows on the topic of their choice Connects to the device's camera roll so that children can customize scenery and puppets with personal images or topic areas Lets children add multiple puppets to any show for collaboration Saves shows to the camera roll to be viewed again or shared	Smartphone, tablet
Draw and Tell	Allows for open-ended projects using drawing and voice recording Connects to device's camera roll so that children can choose to draw on a picture; completed projects can be added to the cameral roll to be viewed again or shared Offers stickers to add to drawings and the option to move the stickers like puppets in recording mode Allows for single or multiple users	Smartphone, tablet
iMovie	Connects to device's camera roll so that children can choose images and/or video Lets children create films with a variety of additions such as music and text Provides for collaboration with storyboard ideas so that children discuss how to best communicate their ideas Lets children share finished films in a variety of ways	Apple desktop/ laptop, smartphone, tablet

Close Ended	Features	Accessible Devices
RAZ Kids	Provides leveled reading passages for children followed by a multiple-choice quiz to test retention of information Provides data on children's performance for teachers with connected accounts	Desktop/ laptop, smartphone, tablet
Bugs and Numbers	Provides a number of different math-based activities with a bug theme (such as tracing numbers, choosing a number that matches the number of objects displayed, and moving a bug left and right) Plays a recording of "Oops!" if a child makes an incorrect answer	Smartphone, tablet
Moby Max	Provides a variety of skills-based practice opportunities that function as a virtual worksheet Lets children drag a choice or write in a blank space and gives feedback on whether the answer is right or wrong Offers a short game as a reward when children earn enough right answers Provides data on children's performance and allows teachers to set goals for timed practice	Desktop/ laptop

Digital Tools for Learning, Creating, and Thinking

Next Steps

1. **Take stock.** Make a list of technologies available to you in your program. List the ways you use these technologies. Do these uses support higher-order thinking (creating, applying, or synthesizing ideas)? Is your use of these technologies project based, collaborative, or creative? Does the technology focus on skills practice? List the apps you use and review the description of open- and close-ended apps provided previously in this chapter. Which apps that you use are open ended? Which are close ended? If you have no technologies, consider what you could acquire and start talking about them with colleagues.

2. **Set aside time to explore technologies yourself.** Many technologies are readily available, but you need time to discover new applications and to get comfortable with a new technology or app before you begin using it with children. Exploration is open ended and, with the vast number of options available, can be time consuming. I suggest giving yourself a set amount of time to explore so that it doesn't get overwhelming. Exploring encompasses a few different methods:

   a. Search for open-ended apps. Sources like Edutopia.org or a community of early childhood educators such as those on NAEYC's HELLO platform can support your search. Even with such tools, be sure to evaluate the usefulness of each app for your own context and the children's interests and needs.

   b. Talk to a colleague or search YouTube for videos on all the functions of a technology you already have or reviews of an app you are curious about.

   c. Play! Spend time trying out the functions of the apps you already have. What can you make? What functions have you never used? Explore with curiosity. Remember that there is no failure in play, just exploration and learning.

Note: There are many free apps, but some do cost money. If an app costs money, look for reviews of the app before purchasing. In addition to YouTube, see the suggested evaluation tools in the list of resources on page 103.

CHAPTER 2

Creating, Collaborating, and Communicating

A Framework for Thinking About Technologies

As discussed in Chapter 1, considering technologies in terms of being open or close ended is helpful for evaluating their usefulness in the classroom. This chapter focuses on three skills that technologies can foster and how those can provide a framework for thinking about integrating technologies into your curriculum. While testing and standardization movements emphasize basic literacy and math skills, children must be able to think critically, think creatively, and problem-solve. Early childhood educators must teach in ways that enable children to develop these skills (Resnick 2017).

I started my work with early childhood teachers thinking about how technologies can be used in developmentally appropriate ways in play-based programs. These teachers were committed to play-based teaching. They knew that technologies were integral to the children's daily lives but also worried that using technologies in their programs would detract from the rich play they saw occurring. However, rather than intentionally choosing technologies that aligned with their beliefs about effective teaching and learning, they were often simply not using technologies. So, I partnered with them to see how technologies could be implemented in developmentally appropriate teaching. Together, we discovered that the teachers could approach learning in a developmentally appropriate way by using apps that allow for creating, collaborating, and communicating. These skills align with the NAEYC and Fred Rogers Center's position statement (2011) on technology and interactive media. In addition, groups like the National Educational Association and International Society for Technology Education identify creating, collaborating, and communicating as critical for learning and participation in daily life and the workplace.

Thinking about creating, collaborating, and communicating as skills that can be fostered by technology use can be helpful for selecting technologies and planning for use, but keep in mind that these skills are not really separate. In fact, they often overlap in one project. The aim of this chapter is not to sort activities by skill but to support teachers in considering the kind of thinking and skills children can develop by using different technologies.

Further, I acknowledge that the technologies available in a classroom or program will vary widely depending on the resources available to teachers and administrators. I have worked in settings where each classroom teacher had several technologies available to use and also with a small program that began incorporating technologies into the curriculum by purchasing one iPad for its two classrooms. The framework presented in this chapter can help teachers and administrators consider how to use existing technologies; it can also help them begin a conversation about planning to include technologies in the classroom, including what kinds of technologies would help meet goals for creating, collaborating, and communicating and what resources are needed to meet those goals. Chapter 7 discusses planning for intentional integration of technologies in the classroom or school and shares some resources to guide that discussion.

Creating

The Lifelong Kindergarten research group, founded by Mitchel Resnick at the MIT Media Lab, is based on Friedrich Froebel's conception of kindergarten, which valued childhood as time of exploration and learning, centered play as an important context for learning, and encouraged creativity (Froebel Trust n.d.). In his research, Resnick aims to foster joyful learning that involves exploration, creation, collaboration, and play and to apply this to learning with technologies. However, he worries that this kind of learning may not be found in all kindergartens anymore. He says, "kindergarten is becoming like the rest of school. . . . I believe the rest of school should become like kindergarten" (2017, 10). One of the aspects Resnick believes is missing from kindergarten is the learning that children do when they use creative thinking in play.

In play-based classrooms, children are given extended periods of time to engage in various kinds of self-directed play, such as block building, painting, playdough, and dramatic play. During these experiences, children use creative thinking to conjure up stories, take on roles in these stories (which builds their working memory and inhibitory control), and problem-solve. For example, as preschooler Milo builds an X-wing fighter jet with hollow blocks, he has to draw on his memory of *Star Wars* for the outline of the ship and then look at the shapes available in the hollow blocks to figure out which will help him build the ship. He has to problem-solve to figure out which blocks will help him make the *X* shape of the wings. He, his friends, and the teacher test out different block combinations to try to achieve a structure that matches the image in his mind. Milo has to use clear communication and social skills to work with friends while building. Then, once he is finished building, he uses creative storytelling skills to begin weaving a story around the X-wing fighter. He and his friends use their working memory to remember this fictional story and practice inhibitory control as they try to stay in their roles and participate in the story. All of the work done in play builds skills critical for later problem solving and critical and creative thinking.

It might seem as if integrating technologies in the classroom would prevent this kind of imaginative play, but the opposite is actually true. Later, Milo took a picture of his creation and audio-recorded a reflection on the work that he did to create it. He shared this picture and audio reflection with his family so that they could talk about it further. This connection with his family encouraged Milo to build more, both at home and at school, and to talk more about what he was doing. Intentionally adding technology use in a program can extend and support children's play.

You can use technologies to support creative play by

1. Providing a space for children to explain and reflect on their nontechnological creations

2. Providing a medium for creating

Using Technologies to Explain and Reflect

Children often engage in focused, creative, and critical thinking in play, but they don't always have a chance to reflect on what they did or to share that work. Reflection is an important process that helps children develop metacognitive skills as they think about how they arrived at a conclusion or solution. It can also be an opportunity to build resilience: Did they do anything that was hard for them? How did they keep going? How did they problem-solve? How did they ask for help? Recognizing how to get through challenges helps children understand that not everything runs smoothly and that they can learn from failures. This can be particularly important for work created with technologies. Because children often only see finished products that look perfect, they may feel like everything done with technologies is seamless and perfect. Reflecting on process helps children see that learning takes place through exploring, observing, thinking, trying, reflecting, and refining.

Here are some suggestions for using technologies to help children reflect on creating:

> **Develop an explain-and-reflect routine:** Technologies such as tablets make it easy for children to take pictures of their creations and record their process. This can become a routine, in which children can choose to capture a painting, building, or project that they are proud of and explain their process. Start the routine by having a teacher support the reflection with questions, and move toward independence as children understand the process.

> **Use a different kind of show-and-tell:** Show-and-tell is an opportunity for language and community building. It does not have to be restricted to objects brought from home. Take pictures of a child's creations, then project the image so the child can explain and answer questions from their peers about their creative process.

> **Share child examples:** Writers often use mentor texts to inspire their work. To apply this with young children, take pictures or videos of play to share with the class. Point out the problem solving, collaborating, or creative thinking that classmates are doing in play and encourage other children to think about how they might use the same skills in their play.

Technologies can support traditional play activities by allowing children to record and reflect on the work done in play.

Digital Tools for Learning, Creating, and Thinking

> **Document learning:** Collect the explain-and-reflect recordings as examples of a child's creative thinking and problem solving. Periodically review to see changes in play and reflection over time. Invite the children to participate in the review. Help them see how much they have grown by looking at a project they made at the beginning of the year and one later on. Emphasize how much more they can do now!

Using Technologies as a Medium for Creating

Technologies can also be the medium children use to make something. Drawing apps allow children to draw with their fingers, often mimicking many different mediums (crayons, markers, paint, etc.), and to record stories of their art. Camera apps also provide video-recording capabilities, which children can use to create their own movies or plays based on stories they invent. Likewise, there are apps that allow children to create and record their own puppet shows, including choosing or making the scenery and puppets. All of these options also offer the opportunity to share stories with an authentic audience because teachers can replay videos or puppet shows for the whole class or share them with families via digital portfolios.

Suggestions for using technologies as a medium for creating include these:

> **Keep it in their hands.** Children take the pictures, draw on the app, or act as the videographers, actors, and speakers. They do the work, and they benefit from the learning. This doesn't mean teachers aren't involved; they are supporting or guiding so that children can learn by initiating and creating.

> **Create a storytelling routine.** Scaffold stories by asking questions or using storyboards, and then have children create and perform the story. Share these stories with the whole class or digitally with families.

> **Create as a class or in small groups.** Many technologies support shared creating, so provide opportunities for children to collaborate, practice sharing ideas, and negotiate roles. Teachers can model or offer support in the creative process.

> **Encourage tinkering.** When children use apps, they often want to press all the buttons to find out what they do. This is a messy but important part of learning. Technologies are not always intuitive, but you can often troubleshoot by trying out functions. Just by exploring, children can discover new functionalities in apps that the teacher thought they knew well. Children also sometimes press a button that erases their picture or covers up their drawing—that has to be okay, too. By encouraging tinkering, you are telling children that it is okay to experiment, explore, and try things, even if it does not work out the way they wanted. It is all part of learning, and these messages are incredibly important for young learners.

> **Share child examples.** As with explaining and reflecting on creating, it's important for children to share what they made and the process of making it with their peers. Sharing allows children to be inspired by and learn from each other. It can support children in seeing themselves and their peers as capable and knowledgeable learners. Children view each other as resources as they work to answer questions and act on new ideas.

> **Focus on the process, not the product.** Technologies can support children in creating products that are impressive. This is both wonderful and potentially harmful because the promise of a perfect product can sometimes stop good work and further creation. Just as it is not developmentally appropriate to edit a child's artwork or insist that every child make the same piece of art, teachers need to, for example, allow children to take imperfectly centered pictures so that they can learn how to focus and adjust a camera. Let them tell stories in their own words so that they can develop vocabulary. Focus together on the process of learning, not the end product.

> **Provide space and time for play.** "Play is, in fact, a complex occupation, requiring practice in dialogue, exposition, detailed imagery, social engineering, literary allusion, and abstract thinking" (Vivian Gussin Paley as told to the American Journal of Play, 2009, 122). It is important to remember the valuable work done in play so that you prioritize time for play. Open-ended apps encourage creation, but if these apps are not part of an environment where children have the space and time to play and discover, the creative opportunities are lost.

Collaborating

What I remember most about the classrooms of my elementary years are the rows of desks that communicated that the classroom was a place where each student would succeed or fail on their own accord—no group work. But education programs ought to reflect the fact that teams of people in a variety of fields have worked together to make discoveries, invent new products, and accomplish major tasks. Today, collaboration between students is valued in many schools. Desks in many classrooms are clustered together or have been replaced by tables so that children can work together on group projects and support each other even in their independent work. Open spaces provide a place for the whole class to meet to work together and enable children to turn and talk to a partner about their thoughts and ideas. Educators understand that children can learn with and from each other.

Technology use in the classroom is not always collaborative, but more and more technologies do allow for collaborative use, such as with simultaneous touch or multiple users accessing the same text at the same time on different devices. This coworking, coauthoring, and collaborating can take place in different ways and in different sized groups.

> In a first grade class, the children discuss the care of their new class pet with the teacher. They are making a book of rules for caring for Edward the bunny. The teacher takes notes as they make a list of rules: "Feed him carrots," "Don't pick him up," and "Be gentle." They talk about the pictures that they will need to take for the book. Children take turns taking pictures and then pass around the tablet to record the audio rules for the book. During this process, they have to remember to listen to each other, be quiet when someone else is speaking, wait their turn, look at the pictures to remember what they are talking about, and prompt another child if they get stuck on what to say.

· · · · · · · · · · · · · · · · · · · ·

In a kindergarten class, two children pass a tablet back and forth as they take turns interviewing each other. They have just participated in a "trash to treasure" project as part of their recycling unit. Jooeun has made a candy machine out of a tissue box and other materials. Daniel has used a paper towel roll to make a rocket ship. One child video-records the other and asks questions such as "What did you make?," "How does the candy come out?," and "What's that button?" Although these children worked independently on their projects, they become partners in reflecting on that work.

. . . .

In a preschool class, a small group of children are creating a story in a puppet app. They work together to decide on characters, setting, and story.

Lacey: First, they were in the city and now they are getting lost and they will go in the forest.

Georgia: (*Looks through the scene options.*) I want the beach.

Lacey: But they are forest characters . . .

Georgia: Right. (*Swipes to the forest scene.*)

As shown in the last vignette, some apps have many choices, and children have to work together to make these choices and stay consistent with the story they want to tell.

Here are some suggestions for encouraging collaboration:

> **Talk about working together.** To work together successfully, young children need support. Before a project starts, talk about how to be a good group member and how to share work. Set guidelines together as part of the class culture.

> **Design projects that offer different roles.** Working together doesn't always mean everyone is doing the same thing together. Projects can be a great place for children to try different roles and practice different skills. Using technologies can introduce new roles that might excite reluctant learners. In Anneliese and Christi's preschool classroom, for example, one child did not want to create a story for a class-wide story-acting routine until he learned that he could choose to be the videographer for his own story. Once he discovered that this was an option, he enthusiastically participated.

> **Look for ways to use technologies as a small part of a project.** When you think about working with technologies, you may think of children sitting in front of a screen, but this is rarely the case anymore because so many technologies are small and easy to carry around. Technologies may be just one small part in a larger project. For example, you might video-record children acting out a story that one child has worked on for days, ask children to look for pictures of different homes around the world for a social studies project, or help them take pictures of a science project over a series of days to document changes they observe. All of these actions are a small part of the overall experience, but they can make a critical difference in the way a group project works.

Communicating

When teachers share children's creations and ideas with families and others in the learning community, families often become more connected to their children's teacher, the children are more connected to each other, and there is a stronger sense of community in the school or program. When it comes down to it, these connections and community follow from communication. Children are building communication skills when they create and collaborate, but they are also communicating their ideas through sharing their work and their days with each other and their families. Teachers can use digital portfolios to upload images and projects the children have created so that this kind of sharing does the following:

> Acknowledges the work children have done and allows them to feel proud

> Creates space for children to learn from each other

> Connects families to classrooms

Supporting Children's Pride in Their Work

Preschooler Ayla bounces into the classroom and announces, "I gonna make a story. It's gonna have a mermaid, a princess, and a witch!" She has been using an app to create digital puppet shows, watching them with classmates in school and sharing them at home. Kindergartner Harley, drawing a picture at a table with friends, turns to an adult and says, "We can take a picture of these, and then we gonna talk and send it to our mommies." These children are each part of a program that uses technologies to share work regularly with families. Having someone pay attention to their work and talk to them about it is powerful for young children. Sharing on platforms such as digital portfolios, classroom blogs, or virtual bulletin boards signals to children that their work is worthy of an audience.

Here are some suggestions for sharing children's work:

> **Tell children when you share their work.** Often, teachers add children's work to folders or to a website without involving the children in this process, and children only find out afterward if their families comment on work sent home. The sharing portion of work done in school can seem disconnected from the work itself. Make this practice more explicit by talking about which projects you are sharing digitally.

> **Give children agency.** Part of building pride in one's work is receiving positive feedback from others, but another important part is recognizing when you have worked hard on something and want to share that with others. Encourage children to make choices about which work they want to photograph and send home or which digital creations they want to add to their portfolios. As they choose, ask them how they made their choices so that they can reflect on the work they have done. Then honor those choices.

> **Allow for multiple ways to share.** Although smart device ownership has continued to grow, some families may be unable to access a digital portfolio or classroom blog. Some blog posts or images can be printed and sent home to families. Teachers can also invite families into the classroom for a time when children share their favorite items from their digital portfolios.

Learning from Each Other

Digital creations and images can be projected on screens and viewed in the same way you might read a piece of writing at the end of a writing workshop. Encourage children to talk about how they created something, what their failures were, what they learned from them, and how they made adjustments or fixed mistakes. This can inspire ownership and pride in their efforts and lets all children learn from what each one shares.

Connecting to Families

Renowned advocate for play Vivian Gussin Paley once told an interviewer, "It is the teacher's role to keep telling anecdotes about how clever, inventive, innovative, nice, and sweet children are in play" (Dombrink-Green 2011, 93). Many teachers have taken up this mantle, but it can be difficult to share children's experiences with families when face-to-face encounters with families are few and newsletters only have enough space for highlights. New technologies enable educators to go beyond anecdotes to share images and recordings of the work children do. When families feel included and informed, they may feel empowered to use technologies to connect to the classroom and perhaps share their own playful anecdotes or family stories with the teachers and other children. Ensuring that technologies are not just used to give families information, but to truly engage families in respectful two-way communication, can help strengthen the home–school connection and enrich the curriculum by helping families feel comfortable with sharing their knowledge and cultural assets.

Next Steps

1. **Evaluate your current uses of technologies.** Do any involve creating, collaborating, or communicating? What opportunities do children have to use these skills?

2. **Choose a focus.** If you are new to using technologies, consider which of these three skills you would like to use as a focal point for integrating technologies. They often overlap—we collaborate on creations that communicate our ideas—so don't worry about separating them. Choosing a focal question, such as "How can I encourage more collaboration?," can help guide changes in your teaching.

3. **Get started with a project.** Technologies can be used for playful purposes, but children often need a jump start before they feel free to play and explore. Design a project so that the whole class can learn the technology and start creating, collaborating, and communicating with support. See Chapter 5 for ideas.

Evaluating Technologies: Can Children Create, Collaborate, or Communicate?

There are multiple ways to create, collaborate, and communicate with technologies—so many, in fact, that it can feel overwhelming. Teachers and administrators evaluate available technologies by considering how each will support these skills. Use the guiding questions below to help you. Chapter 4 provides more specifics about initiating activities and routines with children.

Create

Can children actually create something with this technology?

This simple question is an important one. Perhaps an even more important question is, how much autonomy do children have in creating? Some "drawing" apps limit children to tapping to fill in a preset outlined picture with color rather than using a finger to color as they choose. Similarly, some storytelling apps are filled with "story starters" so that the children must finish a preset story rather than tell their own. Just as with developmentally appropriate artwork, what children create with technologies should reflect their abilities and developmental readiness rather than a ready-made project made by an adult.

Does the technology support or extend the learning done in creating?

A great deal of creative, imaginative, and critical thinking and making happens away from technologies. Just set building materials in front of a group of children, and most adults would recognize the important work that happens in creative play: imaginations start revving, problem solving begins, and collaboration kicks in. Technologies can help children extend this work by documenting and sharing their processes and creations. Children can use many apps to capture images of their work and either write or record their ideas about what they made and how they made it. This supports important reflection and metacognition and marks the work as important enough to share with an audience.

Collaborate

Does the technology support multiple users at the same time?

Tablets and Smart Boards can accommodate more than one user touching the screen, often at the same time. Cloud-based software, such as Google Classroom, allows multiple children to be on one document at the same time but on different devices and even in different places. The ability for multiple children to use an app at once can support and encourage collaboration.

Does the technology allow for different roles?

Beyond multiple hands touching it at the same time, it is important to think about how the technology might be able to foster collaboration by allowing for children to participate in different ways. Can someone be the speaker and someone else be the videographer? Are there different characters in the story? Could someone make the scenes or take the pictures? Assigning or supporting children in choosing roles can encourage participation in an activity, support children's agency, and help children see each other's unique strengths and contributions.

Is the technology appropriate for project-based learning?

This might be the most important question. Projects can be done independently, but collaboration needs a project. Filling out a worksheet together is not really collaboration. Taking turns on a close-ended app supports an important social skill, but it does not really foster collaboration because each child is focused on an individual, rather than a shared, goal.

Communicate

Does the technology allow for children to easily share their ideas with an audience?

Not all technologies or apps allow for easy sharing. One teacher tried a new app to create a class e-book only to realize that the only way for families to access the e-book was to download the app it was created in, connect with the class app via email, and then download the e-book through the app. This was too many steps. Look for technologies and apps that allow projects to be easily saved and then shared via the platform of your choice.

Does the technology allow for multimodal communication?

Look for technologies that provide multiple ways for children to communicate ideas. Many technologies and apps encourage multimodal communication, with options to add text, images, drawings, and recorded voice. Adding layers like this can help build children's understanding.

Does the technology support all learners with a variety of methods of expression?

Communicating with technology also can offer differentiated ways for children to express ideas. Support dual language learners or children with language delays or impairments by looking for apps that mix images with the opportunity to audio-record, play back, and re-record so that they can get audio feedback, rehearsal space, and the support of an image to express their ideas.

While sharing children's work offers many benefits, be sure to align your communication with your program's privacy policies. In addition, see Chapter 6 for ways to harness the positive aspects of sharing work while respecting children's privacy.

PART 2

Developmentally Appropriate Technology Use

CHAPTER 3

Mindsets and Guidelines for Using Technologies

I work with early childhood education alumni from Manhattanville College to host an annual conference for early childhood educators. One year the conference theme was related to science, technology, engineering, arts, and math (STEAM). Our keynote speaker, who ran a children's science center, set up a makerspace and asked presenters to create workshops to actively engage teachers in exploring STEAM. The morning of the conference, I walked the keynote speaker through the makerspace before participants arrived. As we were chatting, we passed by a table of Magna-Tiles™, which are plastic blocks and flat tiles with magnets. Both of us noticed a new arched tile we had never encountered, and we started wondering and exploring. We asked, "How does it connect to the other pieces?," tried it out and then asked, "Would it pick up other blocks, like a horseshoe magnet?," tried that and then wondered, "How many can it hold?" We wanted to know how it worked, so we played with it. Some of our explorations led to what could be described as failure—the magnetic arch wouldn't stick in every direction and couldn't hold more than three blocks—but there is no real failure in play.

When teachers think of play, they see opportunities for exploration and learning. If a child doesn't complete their own goals in the play (for example, the tower they were building falls down or the playdough animal they make doesn't look quite right), most teachers wouldn't label it failure. When the new magnetic tile didn't do something that we thought it might, we learned from that and moved on to the next exploration. I realized that the way we were playing with the tiles is the exact opposite of how many teachers interact with digital technologies, which might be the first thing that needs to change to support child creators.

Technologies are invented to help us do something that we can't do without them. Magnetic tiles are a form of technology. Digital technologies are designed to make things easier, and the way they accomplish tasks can seem almost magical. Depending on your age, perspective, and experiences, they may be something you grew up with, something exciting that you discovered as an adult, or something new, unfamiliar, and possibly uncomfortable. Some people expect using a new device or app to be easy, and when it is not, they often become frustrated and upset. It feels like a failure. Consequently, they sometimes give up and label themselves "not tech savvy." But these same people would never say they are "not block savvy."

A new mindset is essential for integrating technologies into a program. Carol Dweck's (2015) research on learning mindsets has shown that children are affected by the way adults talk about learning and especially about failure and mistakes. Children pick up on the mindsets of the adults around them. Teachers who label themselves "not tech savvy" are communicating to children that they too will either be good with technologies or not, that technologies will always work for them or will always fail them. In a world where technologies are increasingly part of learning, working, and playing, this is a worrisome mindset to create. The mindset for approaching technologies must support teachers and children who are creating, collaborating, and communicating with them.

A Play Mindset

Play is valued as a key component of DAP because it is a critical way young children learn about the world (NAEYC 2020). It's vital to bring a play mindset to learning with technologies. A play mindset has four components: explore; fail; focus on process, not product; and scaffold learning.

Explore

A large part of play is exploration. Preschoolers spend time at the water table pouring water in and through different vessels to see what happens. First-graders take the Unifix cubes from a measuring lesson and stack them to see how tall they can build a tower. Outside, children of all ages run around, looking under rocks for bugs and picking up sticks and acorns to repurpose for imaginative play. Likewise, when you present a child with an app, they are likely to start pressing all the buttons. They want to see all the options, what each button does. They are exploring because they are curious about what the tools can do.

Many adults treat technologies very differently; they view a technology not as a tool to explore but something that will or will not do what they "tell" it to do. This often leads to frustration because when something doesn't work out, it's set up as a failure: the technology "didn't listen" or "didn't work" or "hates me." Technologies don't have feelings; they have been designed for a particular function and can perform that function. This is why mindset is important. When a person uses technology, are they doing so to explore or to accomplish a task without failing? If it is the latter, they may be setting themselves up for frustration.

Even when technology use is not frustrating, failing to explore means potentially missing something. When I first started using an app called Shadow Puppet Edu, I was excited that this app would allow children to take or upload pictures and then record their voices over them. The teacher I was working with was interested in using technology for storytelling, so we introduced the app to the children in her program. I focused on helping the children learn how to take a picture, select it in the app, and record their voices. When the children got the tablet in their hands, they started pressing buttons. They were exploring, and we learned from their explorations: we could zoom in and out on a part of the picture with our fingers, use touch to draw on the picture, or write words over the picture using the button with a *T* on it. These functions were not part of my initial idea of how we would use this app, but they added to the ways children could tell their stories. Their exploration helped all of us learn new uses for the app.

Fail

Two kindergartners are building a tower in the block center. They want to see how high it can get.

Ms. Laurentis: "That tower is very tall! How tall are you going to make it?"

Amir: "So tall, even taller than you!"

The children stack blocks with anticipation, and as the tower gets higher, it starts to sway until finally it falls. The children are momentarily disappointed and at the same time exhilarated by what they had accomplished just moments before.

Ms. Laurentis: "That was a tall tower! I wonder why it fell?"

Asha: "Let's make it even taller!"

Ms. Laurentis: "I wonder if a different shape will help it stay up. Let's look at the architecture book to see if tall buildings have different shapes."

In this scene, you could say the children failed because the tower they were building fell before it was as tall as they wanted it to be. However, I have seen this scenario play out countless times in programs, and the children don't feel like failures. The teachers are never disappointed or frustrated; rather, they see the failure of the tower as a learning experience, an opportunity for children to learn from the first attempt, try again, and learn more. These same teachers, however, often become frustrated when an app does not work. They try a new app, such as one they can use to record a class e-book, but then they make a mistake—forget to save or press record—and they feel like a failure. Rather than try again, they put the app aside until they see me again and ask me to walk them through it.

It would be silly if, when the blocks fell in the previous scene, Ms. Laurentis said, "Ugh, it didn't work—I'll have to call IT" or "What's wrong with these blocks? I'm just not block savvy" or even "When Miss Vicki comes, she'll help us with those blocks." Ms. Laurentis would never say that about blocks because she feels comfortable with using blocks; she has seen blocks fall before and has suggested children try a different way to make a taller tower. Digital technologies are more complicated than blocks, and there are times when you need an expert to fix a piece of technology. However, there are also many times when a different mindset sees failure as an opportunity to say, "That didn't work—I wonder why? I wonder what I can learn by trying a different way." When failure is acceptable, you can learn from it. When you ask, "I wonder why . . . ?," then you can step back to think about what you did, what did and did not work, how to solve the problem, and what you can learn. If this process feels stressful because of past experiences with technologies, apply Dweck's advice: "Anytime you feel the need to say, 'I'm just not a math person,' add the word *yet* at the end" (2015, 23). Perhaps you can try out "I'm just not technology savvy—yet."

Focus on Process, Not Product

Play-based learning focuses on the process as an important part of the learning, even more so than the final product. While open-ended apps provide a playful process for children to create, one challenge is the possibility that a user can create a wonderful product that is visually stunning. This may not seem like a challenge; it may seem like a wonderful aspect of using open-ended apps—why wouldn't you want to have visually attractive products to share with families? However, just because it's possible does not mean it's a developmentally appropriate expectation for what children can do with technologies. When I work with teachers who focus on the product, they tend to keep the technologies in their hands, not the children's, and sometimes decide that a product is not good enough to share with families. These same teachers encourage children to mix colors in finger paint, color outside the lines, use developmental spelling in their writing, drag their hands through the sensory table, and roll and smoosh playdough. They don't do cookie-cutter art projects because they value the process of children's exploring and learning to express themselves more than sending home a perfect-looking project. Yet, even teachers who believe strongly in play-based education may hesitate to share a digital puppet show that contains playful shouts and messy movement. Our own experiences with technology, especially social media, tell us that with technology we can make things perfect. Researchers are questioning whether this is a good thing (Luby & Kertz 2019); many teachers already know that aiming for perfection is not a good thing.

Focusing on the process is a critical part of using creative technologies. Use questions like the following to help you focus on the process and evaluate the learning that is happening even with messy products:

> What are my objectives with using this technology? Did the process meet these objectives?

> If I share this with other children or with families, what learning can I point to?

- Did the child learn how to use a technology? Was it in their hands?
- Did they explore the features of the app? Figure out how to use the app in a way that was new to them?
- Did they create something new? Practice a language skill? Use new vocabulary?
- Did they collaborate with a partner?

Chapter 6 will focus on sharing children's learning and projects through technologies with families. Sometimes families also need help developing a process lens, to see what their child is doing in the messy work of play. Unpacking the process can help families value their children's work as developmentally appropriate.

Scaffold Learning: Digital Natives, Not Digital Wizards

Most young children do not feel that technologies "like" them or do not like them; they learn that idea from the way some adults react to technologies. In addition, because many children have always lived in a world where screens are integrated into daily life, they tend to be curious and comfortable with technologies. This immersion in a world run by technologies is why Prensky (2001) refers to them as digital natives. It is critical to remember, however, that digital natives are not digital wizards. One of the most important factors of the play mindset is that the teachers are able to join children in exploring and creating with technologies. Just because children will more readily press buttons and want to use technologies does not mean they know how to use them without support, nor does it mean that they will make good choices about how to use them. They need teachers to guide and scaffold these experiences.

Think back to the example in the introduction with four children chatting about the different technologies in their lives. They know what technologies are, they have some knowledge about how a tablet works and what people do with it, but they confuse some concepts. Leo calls the passcode a phone number; Carolina says she has Netflix as if it is the same kind of technology as a tablet computer. They hear people talking about technologies, copy motions, learn passcodes, and try to apply the vocabulary they have learned. This is constructivist learning in action; young children are continually taking in information from the world around them and creating new understandings (NAEYC 2020). These are all good skills for learning about the world around them. However, educators also must think about what children don't know and the misunderstandings that have come from learning through observing and coming to their own conclusions. Taking what they know about child development, the specific children they work with, and the context of the classroom and the children, families, and communities, teachers can intentionally design technology learning experiences that allow for engagement, creativity, and playful collaboration that support children in constructing knowledge (Bredekamp & Willer 2022). Without thoughtful, purposeful instruction, children will have a harder time coming to those new understandings and learning how to apply knowledge to technologies use.

Supporting Child Creators

In his well-known TED talk, Sir Ken Robinson asserted that "creativity is as important as literacy, and we should treat it with the same status" (2006). This is certainly a bold claim, and yet it seems to be one that fits many of the early childhood programs I visit where literacy, math, science, art, engineering, and social studies exist alongside or are integrated into play. Play is perhaps the ultimate vehicle for imagination and creativity, where stories are embodied and shouted, structures are built and expanded upon, and art and sensory materials are explored and transformed into something new and unique. I argue that technologies like open-ended apps should be incorporated into this time for play as well; with open-ended apps, children use technology as a medium to express their creativity. This notion can be in stark contrast to the play we often think of when teachers and families think of playing with technologies. That usually conjures up a vision of a child in front of a screen, alone and clicking or pressing buttons (Edwards et al. 2016). In addition, it is likely that the role of technologies in teaching during the

COVID-19 pandemic has affected the ways teachers and families see technologies. Changing the way you view the use of technologies—from clicking to creating—is essential for using technologies as part of DAP.

This is an argument I have made before (Fantozzi 2021; Fantozzi, Johnson, & Scherfen 2018), but I am not alone. Mitchel Resnick of the MIT Lifelong Kindergarten research group is creating playful spaces for children to code with the Scratch program (2017). Even further back, in 1971, Seymour Papert, one of the pioneers of artificial intelligence and leaders in educational technologies, argued in a paper he coauthored with Cynthia Solomon that children should be using technologies to create and problem-solve:

> When people talk about computers in education they do not all have the same image in mind. Some think of using the computer to program the kid; others think of using the kid to program the computer. . . . Why should computers in school be confined to computing the sum of the squares of the first twenty odd numbers and similar so-called "problem-solving" uses? Why not use them to produce some action? (Papert & Solomon 1971, 1)

The paper went on to describe 20 uses for a computer with children, including drawing, composing music, making a movie, and creating a game. Papert labeled this vision of technologies *constructionism* (Papert 1980), a term based in Piaget's constructivism. Papert argued that children would learn about technology and other skills through using technologies to create. Papert went on to develop the Logo system that did go into schools in the 1980s. I used Logo when I was in primary school. Unfortunately, I don't remember Logo as a creative tool; I remember the worksheets I was given with instructions on what commands to enter to make the "turtle" make a shape. This happened in schools across the country: rather than use Logo as a tool for creating, educators focused on using the tool itself. Without a purpose, and given that the computing language was not intuitive, Logo did not have its intended impact in the schools (Resnick 2017). Classrooms did not turn into communities of creators in the 1980s, but we can establish communities of creators in early childhood programs today.

Guidelines

Chapter 1 introduced the idea of intentionally choosing and using open-ended apps in your classroom so that children can be creators with technologies rather than just consumers. Supporting children in becoming creators, however, goes beyond choosing an app. It's important to establish guidelines that will encourage creation and collaboration. As discussed earlier in this chapter, a play mindset for technology is a critical component; educators need to be ready to learn and explore. Chapter 4 will discuss particular teaching strategies to support using technologies in a program, but establishing guidelines for *how* you will approach technologies is an important first step.

It's Everyone's Device

During the first few weeks of the year in Miss Anneliese's preschool class, you are sure to hear a few repeated phrases as she supports the children in learning the routines, rules, and values of the classroom. As she reviews the schedule, you will hear her say, "Then we will have work time," then in a stage whisper, "It's really playtime." She is reinforcing the school value that play is important work in her program and also letting children know that they will have fun. Another phrase you will hear is "Remember, it's not my tablet—its everyone's tablet." This is an important message about the community of creators. Children will see Miss Anneliese use the tablet to lead them in class projects and work one-on-one with them, but she also wants to be clear that the children can come up with their own ideas for using the tablet. Unlocking creativity means that children feel agency to use the technology available for their own purposes. If only the adults use the technology, they are exposing children to technology but not empowering them to use it. Putting the technology in children's hands will help them learn both small lessons, such as not blocking the camera with their fingers, and larger lessons, such as how to imagine something and then use a device to make that idea come to life. In order to learn these lessons, they need to be users, not just consumers.

Putting devices costing hundreds of dollars into the hands of young children can feel unnerving—particularly if acquiring those devices has been difficult and long in coming, as is the case in some programs—but viewing children as capable creators is critical. It's also a learning experience for them. Just as educators want children to learn responsibility in caring for plants, pets, and the general upkeep of the classroom, they can teach children how to take care of technologies. Teach them how to hold the device, turn it on and off, put it away, and if necessary, charge it. Some teachers call this the "Care and Feeding of Technology." Whatever you call it, children need to be taught how to handle devices properly, but these short lessons should not prevent the children from using the tools themselves. Children are capable; it's up to the adults to share the responsibility.

"Must-Do" and "Can-Do"

One constant worry I hear from teachers and families is that once technologies are introduced into the program, it will be impossible to drag children away. With open-ended creative apps, I have found repeatedly that this is not the case. Rather, like in any interest center, some children are very interested in exploring how to create with technologies and others are not interested much at all. This is okay and to be expected. One way to address this is to create "must-do" and "can-do" experiences.

A "must-do" experience is one that the teacher designs for every child to participate in based on educational objectives they all need to reach. These might include

> Making a self-portrait and doing a recording that is "all about me"

> Recording a child talking about something they learned from a family member (for example, mashing plantains or planting flower seeds) over an image sent from home or a drawing

> Recording commentary over pictures of children completing an obstacle course and using descriptive words to talk about how they moved through the course

> Using a drawing app to record their process of solving a math problem

> Participating in a group retelling of a specific book as a part of their book study

> Creating a time-lapse video of their science experiment

Each of these experiences helps teachers assess oral language and understanding of concepts. At the same time, the teachers know that each child is also learning about how to create with technology.

A "can-do" experience is a choice the children can make during center time or independent work time. The basic idea of the experience is introduced to the children, and the teachers occasionally remind the children of the option, but the choice to do the activity is completely up to each child. "Can-do" creative activities might be

> Taking a picture of their artwork and recording their voice describing it

> Taking a picture of toys that they like playing with and sharing why they like them

> Taking a picture of something they built and recording how they made it

> Using a puppet app to make up a story

> Using time-lapse video to record their process of building or making art

> Making a stop-motion video that tells a story

> Recording a video of a story that they and their peers made up

The "can-do" activities send the message to the children that they know how to use this tool, so they can go ahead and use it like any of the other tools in the program. This allows children to try out their skills and invent and use technology in ways the teachers have yet to think up. First-grader Arabella, for example, discovered that the stickers in a drawing app could be used like puppets when she pressed the record button, and she started making puppet stories with friends. Kindergartners Jack and Xavier used the iPad to take pictures of all the birds that came to the bird feeder and then wrote a book called *The Birds of Our School*. Preschooler Arjun recorded an audio recipe for his playdough cookies. "Can-do" activities give motivated children opportunities to explore the technological tools they have learned about in "must-do" activities and use them to create something new.

Technologies can be used to record children's accomplishments. Taking a picture of something a child worked hard at, like this long pattern rope, and recording an audio description of it is a "can-do" activity that many children enjoy during center time.

We Learn from and with Each Other

As the following vignette shows, it's not always easy for young children to work together, but technologies can offer opportunities for learning to do so.

> Preschoolers Georgia and Estefany are huddled around the tablet working on a virtual puppet show. They are using story language like *character* and *setting* and the emergent notions of a plotline. In addition, Estefany, a dual language learner, is gaining English language practice with vocabulary that is important to peer play in the classroom, such as *princesses* and *mermaids*. The two children are practicing digital recording skills: opening an app, pressing a button to start recording, and pressing another to pause. They are also practicing how to work together.
>
> **Georgia:** (*Leans over the tablet.*) Let's see . . . I'm gonna pick . . .
>
> **Estefany:** I want having a mermaid and a princess and a witch.
>
> **Georgia:** (*Continues leaning over and swipes past the mermaids without responding to Estefany.*)
>
> **Miss Vicki:** Hmm, Georgia, remember that you and Estefany are both making this story. I wonder how you might both work together to choose the characters.
>
> **Georgia:** (*Looks at Estefany.*) Do you like this one? It can do fire. (*Presses on the dragon puppet and makes it shoot fire.*)
>
> **Estefany:** Ooh. Yes, you gonna pick that and I'm gonna pick a princess. A dragon gotta have a princess sometimes.
>
> **Georgia:** They can be in the forest, see? (*Swipes to a background.*)

Open-ended apps offer the opportunity for collaboration, but young children often need support as they learn to collaborate. In the vignette above, Georgia is very interested in the app and the story and isn't quite skilled in collaborative storytelling, but with a little prompting from a teacher, she is able to start to work with Estefany. A core consideration of DAP (NAEYC 2020) is recognizing children's individual interests, strengths, abilities, approaches to learning, and challenges and supporting them in moving beyond their current levels of development and learning. Knowing the children you work with is key to supporting their collaboration. Children who know how to collaborate but get lost in their own ideas for a story, like Georgia, benefit from an adult's prompting them back to something they already know.

Creative and collaborative technologies can also support social and emotional skills for children who have difficulty playing or working with others. Story-focused apps, like puppet show apps, require children to listen to each other and take turns, much like in dramatic play, in order to successfully tell a story. Teachers can use children's motivation to explore technologies to scaffold interactions. For example, David, a preschooler in Anneliese's class, did well in all academic areas—for example, he identified all of the letters of the alphabet, could count to 100 and beyond, and had a large vocabulary—but he needed support in working with others. He wanted to control the narrative in play and would end up in disagreements with other children, so he often chose to play alone. David enjoyed using the iPad but would usually use it for creating on his own. Anneliese used his interest in and skills with the iPad to encourage David to join in on collaborative play with the iPad. One day, after seeing Asia pick up a play microphone and pretend to be a newscaster, Anneliese suggested that Asia, David, and a few others could use the iPad to make a video newscast. This set off a project that involved making sets and taking turns being the newscaster or interviewer. David's family often listened to NPR at home, so he enthusiastically joined in. With minimal prompting from Anneliese ("Let's make sure that everyone gets to use the microphone if they want to" or "I think Asia is trying to share her idea for a story; let's listen"), he was able to collaborate with his classmates. David also got to draw from his experiences listening to the news to help his friends, telling them, "Let's say there is a hurricane coming, and when they say that they always talk about what the governor is going to do. I'll talk about the governor. I hear him all the time."

Other children might benefit from a social story, which illustrates examples of behaviors that children are familiar with but that are removed from their own experiences. For example, a teacher might use puppets to act out behaviors such as not sharing the tablet or insisting that the others always do what one puppet wants to do on an app. Children can watch these situations, consider how the puppets might feel, and then suggest ways the puppets can collaborate, even offering phrases that the puppets could say. The important aspect of each of these approaches is that collaboration, an important goal in the classroom, is supported.

Next Steps

1. **Evaluate your own technology mindset.** Is it a play mindset? If you have labeled yourself "not tech savvy," start adding the word *yet* to that phrase.

2. **Start exploring technologies on your own.** Changing your mindset is a process, so begin this process by exploring an open app, and perhaps failing, on your own before you start modeling for the children.

3. **Plan ahead.** As you are exploring new apps, start thinking about "must-do" and "can-do" opportunities for children to create on their own.

"Let's Be Troubleshooters"

Troubleshooting is problem-solving an issue with digital technologies using logic and exploration. Rather than get frustrated when a problem arises, a teacher can say, "Let's be troubleshooters," and use the problem as a teachable moment. During the COVID-19 pandemic, online schooling forced many teachers into troubleshooting mode when a technology suddenly did not work as they had planned. For example, a third grade teacher thought aloud in front of the children when she needed to troubleshoot with technology; this simple strategy enabled the children to know that the teacher noticed something was not right and understand what she thought she might try. This strategy also created space for the children to offer solutions. For example, one day during an online lesson, a video the teacher had planned to show to the class was not working.

Ms. Dehn: Can you all see the video? It seems like it's frozen on my end.

Liam: It's frozen.

Ms. Dehn: Okay, I am not sure why—it worked when I checked it this morning, but that was a while ago. I am going to click refresh to see if it needs to be reloaded, and we'll see what happens. I'll need you to tell me if it's working. But I only need one person to talk at a time. Camila, can you tell me what you see?

Camila: It's still frozen. My dad always says the internet is so slow.

Zaniah: Ms. Dehn, the other day the art teacher said her video didn't work and then she was like, "I will use Chrome," and it did work.

Ms. Dehn: Thanks, Camila and Zaniah. I think my connection is fine, but that can sometimes make videos slow. There is no storm here, so it should be good. Zaniah, I will try to change my browser—thanks for the suggestion. Class, if that doesn't work, I have another activity planned, but let's just try one more thing. Thank you for your patience and for helping me try to figure this out.

The way Ms. Dehn calmly thought aloud about what she could do modeled her troubleshooting process and invited the children to share solutions. Beyond the pandemic, troubleshooting a technological issue might feel less urgent as there will likely be other in-person options for continuing with a lesson. Consider an issue with technology a teachable moment and continue to be a troubleshooter along with the children. In troubleshooting, some key questions can help lead to a solution.

1. **What did you do?** There are times when you know exactly what you did and why something did not work. Maybe you forgot to hit record or accidentally hit delete. This is an opportunity for you to teach something important to the children you work with: it's okay to make mistakes! Notice the mistake, stop, and acknowledge that it caused an outcome you did not want, and then think aloud about what you can do next time.

2. **What have you done before that worked?** Many people have experienced a technology expert's advice to turn off their device when it's not working properly and then turn it back on. This might seem silly, but it is similar to all the blocks falling down and starting again, except that the digital technology is doing some of the early building as it resets. Try it and see what happens. There are other times when you can think back on a successful attempt and run through the steps you took to see if there is something you might have missed or if there's something new to try. This is also an opportunity to build collaboration and community. The teacher does not always have to be the lead troubleshooter. You might say, "Lorenzo had this problem the other day. Why don't you ask him what he did to fix it?" Reliance on each other helps build community, pride, and the idea that every member of the class can be successful with technology.

3. **Are there other things we can try?** Sometimes troubleshooting is necessary not because a technology isn't working but because you are not sure how to do something. This is a great opportunity for exploration and trial and error. For example, you might look at the drop-down menus, try some buttons you have not used before, and observe the results. When you say, "I'm not sure, let's try and see what happens," you are also modeling an important mindset for the children. This tells them they don't always have to have the answer or know the next step.

4. **Where can you learn?** Many websites can help you learn from others' knowledge and experiences. This openness to learning is also an important part of failing. Sometimes you cannot figure it out on our own; you need help. Again, this is an important part of learning about technologies for children. They need to see adults going to FAQ pages and searching for support or talking to tech support. If teachers don't share how to find support, they are hiding part of the experience of failure—figuring out where to get help when you realize you can't do something on your own. If you do need an outside expert, view it as a learning experience. Often when I see a tech support person come to help, they do their work quietly while everyone else is engaged in something else, and then they come over to report that the issue is fixed and leave. In this scenario, no learning has happened! It's a missed opportunity for you and the children to ask questions and say, "We are troubleshooters, and one of the things we do is try to remember what worked last time. Please tell us so that we can remember and learn how to solve the problem on our own if it happens again."

CHAPTER 4

Teaching with Technologies

One of my first experiences with teaching young children how to use an app came unexpectedly. School was closed, and my sons and I were visiting a family friend and her children at the local home goods store she owns. While we were there, a client walked in. I whisked all the children into a back room so my friend could work. Suddenly I had two 6-year-olds, a 5-year-old, and a 3-year-old to entertain, and I was not sure how long the client would be there. Luckily, I had seen a presentation at a recent educational conference from a teacher who used a stop-motion app to help children retell stories. During the presentation, we were encouraged to download the app on our phones, so I did so and explored it during the session. Now, I decided to teach the boys how to use the app, and I scrounged in my bag for materials: gum wrappers, scrap paper, and pens.

First, I introduced the concept of the app by making a short movie using the pens. I told the children my purpose: I wanted to make it look like the pens were walking to meet each other and then dancing. I demonstrated that, by moving my pens bit by bit and taking a picture after each small movement, I could use the app to play the pictures together and make it seem as if the pens could move. The boys were thrilled and wanted to make their own movies. First, we brainstormed story ideas, and then they got to work folding wrappers into mini paper airplanes and scrunching up papers to look like explosions. They took turns being the story director, taking pictures, and making small movements with the items. They learned from each other. They realized that they shouldn't have their foot or hand in the camera view and began to check for that before they took a picture. Each movie got more detailed as they built on each other's stories.

The first movie was simple, just the plane crashing, but by the last movie, they were adding and removing a strip of paper between shots to make it look as if the plane was shooting a laser. I acknowledged their successes ("When you made the plane go up a little and then down, it really looked like it was flying"), commented on challenges ("You want to make it look like an explosion, but that crumpled paper doesn't look like you want it to. Could you color it? Or use a different material?"), and supported them in sharing their finished works with each other ("Say one thing that you liked about their movie and that you might try in yours"). Almost an hour later, when my friend returned, the boys were still engaged in the videos and excited to tell her what they learned.

Gradual Release of Responsibility Model

As discussed in Chapter 3, children can build a play mindset by exploring apps, pressing new buttons to find out how they work and how to create with them. However, although some children can navigate a new app and come up with ideas for creative projects on their own, many need instruction on how to use a new technology or the support of a teacher-designed project before they start creating on their own. When the children and I were in the back of my friend's store, I leaned on a model I had used many times before in my teaching career: the gradual release of responsibility (GRR) model. Introduced by Pearson and Gallagher in 1983, the GRR model is sometimes better known by the phrase "I do, we do, you do" and is based in Vygotsky's notion of scaffolding instruction from introduction of a concept or a skill to independent use (Webb et al. 2019). Often used in literacy workshops, the GRR model can be especially useful in scaffolding integration of technology into a program.

The GRR model has three phases of learning as the responsibility (or ownership) of learning shifts from the teacher to the children: modeling (I do), guided practice (we do), and independent practice (you do).

Modeling

In the first phase of GRR, the teacher explicitly models a skill or concept. The modeling phase is not meant to center learning on the teacher; rather, reflecting Vygotsky's (1978) understanding of learning with others, the teacher shares an experienced user's thought process. The key to this phase involves think-alouds, a method in which the teacher reflects on the cognitive process of a skill and shares that thinking with the children. For example, when Michelle started using technologies in her special education preschool classroom, she focused on increasing opportunities for the children to develop expressive language. She used the tablet to record a whole class reflection about some special visitors who had come to their classroom and modeled her thinking as the class talked about what had happened.

> **Miss Michelle:** Friends, yesterday we had special visitors. Do you remember?
>
> **Ethan:** It was a chinchilla!
>
> **Miss Michelle:** Yes, that's right! We had animals come to our classroom so we could learn about them. I took pictures, and today I want to use the iPad to talk about that visit so your families can learn about the animals, too.
>
> **Leo:** Miss Michelle! I have two iPads at home. Put it on the purple one.
>
> **Miss Michelle:** Your families can see it on that, or on a phone or computer too even if you don't have an iPad. Let's think about the visit: what animals were there?
>
> *(The children call out answers, which Miss Michelle writes down.)*

Miss Michelle: You all remembered so much. Today I want you to think about describing the animals and thinking about what you learned. When I look at this picture of the tortoise, I remember its shell felt hard but also smooth, so I think I am going to say, "The tortoise shell felt hard and smooth" so our families will know what it was like since they weren't there. Now I know what I am going to say, so I will hit the red "record" button and say it.

As Michelle uses the tablet, she is modeling the process of first thinking about what to say and then pressing the record button. Her focus for the content is how to use descriptive language. In the modeling phase, teachers can think aloud the steps of utilizing the device or app as part of the process of completing a project. (I don't advocate for lessons that are solely focused on teaching the uses of a device; without applying the knowledge, learners often forget the steps of the process.) Modeling can also be a great time to support children who don't have access to technologies at home and may not be as familiar with app or device use. If a child is very unfamiliar with a technology, a teacher can provide extra support during guided practice or independent work. When planning lessons with technologies, consider what the children might need support with to determine your focus for the lesson. Do they need support using the technology? Developing new content understandings? Reflecting on the process? See the Making Intentional choices section for more information on these types of lessons.

Guided Practice

During the second phase of the GRR model, the teacher and children work together on the skill that is the focus of the lesson. The teacher is slowly building up children's skills and confidence, so the guided practice phase should have the same objective as the modeling phase. In lesson plans, novice teachers often aim to model one skill but then add on new skills in guided practice, as if completing a list: "I talked about how to reflect on my voice recording—check! Now I'll ask the children to make sure to add details." Modeling is only one exposure to a new concept; guided practice is the children's opportunity to try it.

Guided practice provides an opportunity for children to practice a new skill that has been modeled.

After Michelle modeled her example, she invited the children to record for the class book. By doing this, she gave the children an opportunity to practice what she had just modeled and receive feedback on their attempts.

> **Miss Michelle:** The chinchilla! What do we want to say about the chinchilla? What did it feel like?
>
> **Carson:** It was warm.
>
> **Miss Michelle:** It was warm. Do you remember what the guide said about its fur? What did she call it? Do you remember it was a little silly because it sounded like clothes?
>
> **Carson:** A thick coat of so warm fur! So soft!
>
> **Miss Michelle:** Okay, so do you want to say, "It had a thick coat of soft, warm fur"?
>
> (*Carson nods and records this phrase.*)

Independent Practice

In the independent practice phase of the GRR model, children are invited to work on their own. Depending on your access to technology or program approach, this can be during a whole class time where everyone has a "must-do" activity (a task that each child will complete) or an invitation during independent work time for a "can-do" activity (a task that the children can choose to do). Michelle had only one tablet, so rather than require everyone to record using the same app and descriptive language, she offered an invitation: "Friends, if you have something you want your families to see at home, you can take a picture of it, think about how you can describe it, and then record what you want to say." The children could accept this invitation during center time if they wished. Sometimes, Michelle or one of her assistant teachers will offer an invitation again for children who they feel might need some encouragement (for example, "You worked really hard on that playdough—do you want to talk about it on the iPad?").

An important part of independent practice is that the teacher gives feedback and coaching. When Carolina later wanted to record a reflection about something she built, Michelle offered support:

> **Carolina:** I made something with my Lego.
>
> **Miss Michelle:** What was the something that you made?
>
> **Carolina:** I made a flower and I love it.
>
> **Miss Michelle:** Oh, how lovely! Tell me about the colors.
>
> **Carolina:** It's pink and green and blue and yellow.

In Anneliese's preschool class, the teachers and I introduced the idea of using the tablet as an audio journal. I modeled the process for the children using an app to take a picture of a drawing just like the ones they had done in their journal. Then I recorded a story about it.

Miss Vicki: I've been watching you all write during journal time.

Tyree: I wrote about Ghostbusters!

Miss Vicki: I know, I heard you tell that story! At journal time, you all think of stories, draw pictures, and sometimes write letters too. Then you can choose to come to a teacher and ask them to write your story in your journal. So I wondered, what if there was another choice? I know we use the iPad to write class books, so I thought we could also use the iPad to record our journals. Let me show you. (*Displays the journal drawing.*) I drew this in a journal at work time. I'm going to take a picture of the journal. I'll use the camera app and press the red button when I am ready. (*Picks up the iPad, takes a picture of the journal drawing, and shows it to the group.*) Is this good?

Children: No, you can see your finger!

Miss Vicki: Right, thank you. I need to remember to look at the picture and make sure I can see the whole journal page before I press the red button. (*Repositions the iPad and takes the picture.*) Next I am going to use the same app we used to make our book about the class rules. (*Opens the app.*) I'll choose the picture I just took.

Georgia: From the camera roll.

Miss Vicki: Yes, you remembered! I need to find my picture in the picture library, which is sometimes called the camera roll, and then I can record. First, I'll look at my picture and think of my story. I drew bears, so I think I am going to talk about bears going into the woods on a picnic. When I am ready, I will press the start button and then start talking. (*Models a short story.*) Then I press stop when I am done. So later today, if you want to try recording your story you can come over to me at journal time.

In this case, I provided guided practice to the children who chose to complete this project, which was a "can-do" activity. Some children came up to me the first day; others tried using the iPad for journaling even days later or chose not to use this option. The guided practice was similar whether they chose to do it immediately or on another day. As needed, I offered prompts to guide the children, such as

> "Ready to take your picture? Make sure you can see all of your drawing."

> "Open the app and find your photo."

> "Think about your story before you press record. You can look at your drawing to help support your ideas."

> "You pressed stop. Are you done with your story? Or do you have more you want to say about [story topic]?"

> "When I listen to your story, I want to hear more about [aspect of story]. I wonder if you can add some more details about that."

Finally, the independent work phase came in subsequent journal sessions when children had become comfortable with the procedure and could record their journal entries without prompting.

These three phases are sometimes completed in order within a single lesson, but they do not have to be. Sometimes, a child has started an idea independently but then needs teacher modeling to address a challenge they are having so that they can finish. It is important for teachers to be flexible and respond to children's needs (Webb et al. 2019).

Save Time for Sharing

Set aside time for children to share their work with each other. Sharing can be a powerful tool when used intentionally and with individualized scaffolding. Chapter 6 discusses sharing with families to build community, but when children share their work within the program, especially their choices in independent work, they may inspire other children to try something new. Sharing within the classroom allows for recognition of a child's work without the pressure of needing a device or internet connection at home. Teachers can also talk about process when a child shares their work as well as highlight finished work. If a child has persevered or made a discovery through exploring, other children can learn from that experience.

With this in mind, it's critical that you intenionally plan opportunities for sharing just as you do other aspects of teaching. Many teachers have moved away from sharing because it's poorly planned. For example, young children are active learners, yet teachers sometimes ask them to sit and listen as 15 or more children get two minutes or more each to share. This is simply too long. Even if sharing is a regular part of your classroom practice, the whole class doesn't have to share at one time; you can choose a few children to share one day and assure the others that they will get a chance another day.

Another issue is that listening, like other skills, needs to be taught. Give children specific guidelines about how to listen and respond to their peers. As during show-and-tell, listening to a peer and asking them questions can be great practice in verbal, social, and emotional skills. Support children as they learn how to ask a question or make a comment that is on topic.

Including All Children

Technologies can support children with disabilities or dual language learners in a variety of ways. Often when I speak with teachers about technologies as a support, they first think of assistive technologies, such as e-books that can read the text or augmentative communication apps with symbols that a child selects to "speak" the corresponding word. These technologies play an important role for some children, but some features of open-ended apps can support children with disabilities or dual language learners as they work on the same projects as their peers. For some children, using technologies in the same ways as all children in the class, rather than the technology being something that only they use, can be motivating. Common app features that are particularly supportive are visual images and audio playback.

Visual Images

Many open-ended apps used in early childhood programs have access to the device's camera function to allow the children to integrate visuals and record their voices over photos they have taken. Remember, using photos gives children authentic connection to the projects. These apps also have visual cues that provide scaffolding for children who have challenges with recall or who are learning a new language. For example, when Brandon, a preschooler who needed speech support and had attention challenges, would do a view-and-review activity with his teacher, Debbie, the photo helped him focus on the task and remember the activity. In the following example, Debbie talks with him as he looks at a photo of a painting he made at the easel. They refer to the painting as they talk, and Debbie supports Brandon's language through reciprocal talk as she repeats what he says and then extends his statements.

Brandon: I paint. I make a castle.

Miss Debbie: You painted, and you made a castle with the paints.

Brandon: Yeah.

Miss Debbie: Tell me about the colors you used to make the castle.

Brandon: Yellow, blue, and red!

Miss Debbie: You used yellow, blue, and red. You mixed all the colors together. (*Points to the brownish-purple hue in the picture.*) That is the color that you got.

Brandon: Right!

Feedback

When Arjun first joined his preschool, he did not talk at large group time. His teachers also rarely heard him speak to peers during center time. While they understood that dual language learners with no peers who speak their home language often have periods of silence, they wanted to provide opportunities for Arjun to practice speaking. They found these opportunities using the tablet. Arjun liked to hear his voice recorded on the tablet and would choose it at center time. In fact, one of the first English phrases he spoke to his teachers was, "I do iPad." One of the app features that was most supportive to Arjun was the audio playback. With this feature, the user can record words over a visual image and also pause the recording to listen to what was recorded so far before continuing. Arjun used the recording and playback function repeatedly, and it seemed to offer helpful feedback and also rehearsal time where he could talk, then pause, hear what he had already said, and think about what he would say next. The following vignette illustrates a typical interaction and demonstrates how the audio playback provided scaffolding for Arjun.

Arjun: (*Looks at a picture of his hand pressing playdough and presses "record."*) And press it. (*Presses "stop."*) Let's listen.

Miss Vicki: Okay, let's listen to what you have said for your recipe so far.

(*Arjun and Miss Vicki listen and watch as his voice plays over a series of pictures showing the steps for making a playdough cookie: "A recipe, and roll it, and press it."*)

Miss Vicki: Hmmm, what next?

Arjun: (*Presses "record."*) And . . . (*Hesitates over a picture of his hand pressing a cookie cutter into the playdough.*)

Miss Vicki: (*Presses "pause."*) What will you say here? What are you doing? Do you remember what that is called? You are using a cookie cutter to make the shape. Could you say, "Use a cookie cutter"?

Arjun: (*Presses "record."*) Use the cutter! (*Presses "stop."*) Let's listen.

In this vignette, Arjun knew what he wanted to say and had listened to his voice speaking successfully in English by using the replay button. He went through a loop of speaking in English and enjoying the feedback of hearing himself on the replay. As he started to record the next part of his recipe, he got stuck on a new English vocabulary word: *cookie cutter*. I noticed that he was stuck and supplied it for him, and then he could go on successfully. I could see the pride in his face as he listened to his voice speaking the English he was quickly learning. Hearing himself use new vocabulary gave him almost immediate positive reinforcement. Because Arjun was in a multiage classroom, I worked with him for two years and witnessed his transition to bilingual fluency. As he gained progress in English and comfort in the class, he recorded less often on the tablet, and when he did record, he stopped asking for the scaffold of listening to the recording at each step.

Engagement

Most children are delighted to hear their words recorded and replayed on a tablet. They are also excited to see themselves in pictures, often smiling and pointing. Sometimes, the ability to record their voice or to see a picture of themselves can motivate some children who don't often speak otherwise. At an open house night for families in a special education preschool classroom, Devante, who had developmental delays and rarely spoke or actively engaged with others, started jumping up and exclaiming, "That's Devante!" when his picture came on the screen.

Matthew is a good example of a child for whom technology—specifically an open-ended app rather than assistive technology—supported collaboration, communication, and engagement. Matthew, a preschooler in Debbie's class, received speech therapy services for delayed language development and articulation. He seemed reluctant to talk in class. His speech therapist tried an augmentative communication app on a tablet that allowed him to select from a series of pictures to form a sentence, and then the tablet would "speak" the sentence for him. Matthew did not use this app unless prompted to do so by a teacher. He was, however, interested in using the tablet the same way the other children in his class were, such as taking pictures of their creations and then recording descriptions of their work. Matthew enjoyed talking about the structures he built for his firetrucks and trains. He also was very motivated to do any activity with his best friend, Jorge, so when Debbie's class was reading and retelling the folktale *The Gingerbread Boy*, Jorge and Matthew recorded their retelling together. Here is an excerpt from their retelling:

Miss Debbie: So, tell us about the story *The Gingerbread Boy*. What happened? Who lived in the house?

Jorge and Matthew: The old lady and the old man.

Miss Debbie: And what did they do? They put the gingerbread boy into . . .

Jorge and Matthew: The oven.

Miss Debbie: What did he do? When he was done baking, they opened the oven and . . .

Matthew: He jumpin'!

Jorge: He jump in the oven.

Miss Debbie: He jumped out of the oven and he . . .

Jorge: Out the door!

Miss Debbie: He ran out of the oven and down the street and . . .

Jorge: And the cows come to eat him.

Miss Debbie: He was chased by a cow . . .

Matthew: A cow, a horse, the pig!

In this vignette, Matthew worked with his best friend and teacher to retell the story. He participated enthusiastically, sometimes talking at the same time as his friend and sometimes being the first one to jump in and give an answer. The technology, as well as the chance it gave him to collaborate with others, motivated him to use his vocabulary and comprehension skills to tell the story.

Including All Voices

A culturally sustaining and inclusive classroom includes media that does not just let all children hear their own voices but also gives them the opportunity to see a diversity of abilities and cultural heritages represented in many ways. Broughton and McClary (2020) suggest using video chats to connect to a diverse set of professionals in the STEAM fields and to access images from art and architecture from many cultures (such as exhibits from the National Museum of African American History and Culture or images of structures like the Great Wall of China) to incorporate into the curriculum. Hoffman and Cipollone (2021) partnered with families to create a culturally sustaining and community-responsive listening center for a child care center. They first spoke to and surveyed families about favorite stories, songs, and books. They then gathered these materials and invited families to come to an open house and use a tablet to make recordings for children to listen to in class. Sometimes the families added to a story with their own cultural references and sometimes they read a book in their home language (for example, a father read *Freight Train*, by Donald Crews, in English and in Spanish).

Technologies are sometimes perceived as difficult to use or as things that disconnect us from our communities. Certainly both of those things can be true, but ultimately technologies are tools, so it is up to teachers and administrators to make intentional choices to use technologies in developmentally appropriate ways. Providing supportive modeling and guidance, as well as thinking about possibilities for children to create, collaborate, and communicate with these tools, can help support a culturally sustaining, developmentally appropriate classroom.

Having families record their favorite stories, songs, or books is one way for them to share their cultural heritage with all the children.

Next Steps

1. **Think about your past experience using the GRR model.** Are you familiar with and do you use the model in other areas of instruction? How have you successfully implemented it?

2. **Consider how you can use the GRR model with the children you work with.** Looking at your daily schedule, for example, when can you model a lesson, provide guided practice, support independent practice, and provide a time to share?

What Type of Technology-Related Lesson Do the Children Need?

At times, young children need lessons on how to use technologies, and at other times, they need lessons on the process of making decisions as they are creating and collaborating. On other occasions, lessons center on content learning through the use of technologies. The modeling teachers provide to support learners depends on the children themselves but also on the type of lesson. It's important that teachers pay close attention to what children know and what they might be ready for next (NAEYC 2020).

Technology-use lesson

Using the technology itself should not be the goal of all technology-related lessons. However, once you identify the purpose for using a particular technology, you do need to teach children how to use it. This can be done through intentional teacher modeling with the whole class, but the children's goals or challenges that arise during play also offer wonderful opportunities to model ways that technologies can help children solve the problems they encounter.

Process lesson

The processes of creating and collaborating can be messy. They can also be opaque to young children. Adults have learned over a lifetime how to choose an idea for a project, think about what they need to do to start, work with others, and so on. Process-focused lessons enable teachers to support children in thinking about the processes they need to be successful.

Content-focused lesson

In these lessons, the technology is a means to achieve a learning goal. The design of the lesson and the teacher modeling are focused on those goals.

Table 2 outlines the goal of each type of lesson, examples of possible topics relevant to each type, and sample modeling phrases that might be used.

Table 2. Types of Technology Lessons

Goals	Examples of Lesson Topics	Examples of Teacher Modeling
Technology-use lesson		
To support children in the basic use of a new technology or advanced use of a familiar one	How to hold a device to take a picture	"I want to take a picture of my drawing, but I keep seeing this big thing in the way. Oh, I am holding my thumb in the wrong place!"
	How to zoom in and out on an image	"I want to make sure I get the whole structure in the picture. When I stand here, it is too close, so I need to back up."
		"The other day Xavier wanted everyone to see the spider we took a picture of outside, but it looks very small in the picture. One thing I showed him was, if I do a reverse pinch, then I can zoom in on the spider. Xavier, can you show everyone how you did that? If you want to zoom in on a picture, you can do that too."
	How to start and pause a recording	"I'm recording my recipe. First, I am going to think about the step I want to say for this picture. Once it's in my mind, I'll press this triangle or play button to start recording. I try to be ready with what I want to say, but sometimes I forget! I know that if I can't remember what I wanted to say, I can press this button and it will pause so I can think."
Process lesson		
To help children practice the skills and thought processes needed for creating and collaborating	Coming up with an idea for a project	"I want to share what the field trip was like, and our families weren't there, so I think a class book with pictures of the day might help them see it."
	Thinking about the steps of a project	"I want to be sure that I have all the steps of the recipe, so I need a picture of every step."
	Reflecting on the quality of a project	"When I am acting in a story, I think about the words and then use my body and voice to pretend like I am the character."
	Working collaboratively	"I want to make sure that everyone can hear me, so let's see which is the best voice to use. I'll practice some and you can help me think about how loud I should be when I record."
		"I want to work together with my partner, but if we talk at the same time, we can't understand each other. So, we need to take turns."
	Troubleshooting	"I feel frustrated that this didn't work the way I thought it would, but I know if I think about our troubleshooting process, I can figure it out."
Content-focused lesson		
To use technology as a method for learning another skill or exploring a particular content area	Various topics related to the objective	"When I say my recipe, I am going to use words like *first* and *next*, and at the end I will use *last*. Then everyone will know what part of the recipe we are in."
		"Sometimes math problems are told in stories. We can even make the math problem into a puppet show. I can say, "Four mermaids swam to shore to see if they could find a friend" and add four puppet mermaids to my scene. Now I need to add some action. I think I will make this a subtraction story. I'll say, "But then one mermaid was frightened and swam home" and make that puppet leave the scene. Now how many are left?"

CHAPTER 5

Creating and Collaborating with Technologies

When you begin to use open-ended apps in the classroom, it can be challenging to envision what children might do with them. This chapter offers a few ideas for projects that can be effective with young children. This list is by no means exhaustive, but these projects allow for many different topics and concepts, so they are a good place to start your journey creating and collaborating with technologies.

View and Review

Some readily available technologies—such as tablets, smartphones, and even laptops—let users capture a creation or an event with the camera feature, which can add a powerful step to much of the experiential learning done in early childhood programs. In programs using developmentally appropriate practice, children have many opportunities to create, explore, observe, and learn that do not necessarily involve making a product. Children look closely at nature on the playground or on a walk, build structures, or create with playdough, often with no record of the learning involved. Photographing these explorations and creations offers children an opportunity to reflect on their learning and build expressive language.

Many early childhood educators start with open-ended apps that allow children to take a picture and then record their voice over it because this action builds on what the group is already doing. For example, many teachers already review and talk about a group experience such as cooking or a field trip. In addition, pictures support children's recall of a previous event or project. Most young children need some help remembering events or steps in a process; the pictures act as a prompt so children can focus on using new vocabulary words or other oral language goals. Using an app's text feature, children can practice emerging print skills, such as writing their names, or phonetic skills, such as sounding out and writing words using developmental spelling. Finally, since young children are generally motivated to talk about themselves, capturing their own work or experiences gives them a subject to discuss while supporting language skills and memory. They can then continue the conversations at home with an authentic audience (their families and friends).

A view-and-review project can be done with almost any experience that involves a process, but the following sections discuss some experiences for which it works particularly well.

Playful Creations

Children learn a great deal from constructive play such as building with blocks and other materials or exploring art materials. This play is an excellent opportunity for building focus, executive function, and problem solving. When you take a picture of something children have made and record them talking about it, they build on their learning by verbalizing their processes. This is a great opportunity for oral language development as well as metacognition. The children can use descriptive language for colors, sizes, and shapes and comparison words such as *faster*, *slower*, *heavier*, and *biggest*. They can share their creative and problem-solving processes: How did they build a carrier for their toy turtle? How did they make that microphone for their band? What materials did they use? What story did they invent to go along with their creation? To get started, teachers can model this process, provide prompting questions if needed, and offer children the opportunity to take a picture and talk about their creations.

Technology can help children build on the learning they experience during play and other hands-on activities, such as when they photograph their work and describe it to others.

Class E-Book

In many apps, multiple pictures can be loaded in a chosen sequence with recorded voice or text overlaying the pictures. Teachers can use these apps to create class e-books in which children view and review whole-class experiences or topics that the group is studying. You might make books that reflect on field trips, retell a recipe, share what the class has learned about a topic, review program rules or procedures (such as the care and feeding of a class pet), and more. An e-book is a tool for everyone to review and reflect on shared experiences. Further, it offers an opportunity to practice important collaborative skills such as listening, sharing ideas, and turn taking.

Story Retelling

Retelling is a common practice in building early comprehension. In Chapter 4, Debbie supported Matthew and Jorge in retelling the story of the gingerbread boy. You might take photos of a picture book's pages and record children retelling the story over those photos. Children can be motivated to record a retelling of the story, using the page photos as scaffolding, by the prospect of sharing it with an audience later. In addition, teachers can use a recorded retelling as documentation.

During storytelling, be mindful of your cultural expectations of storytelling and retelling. Research has shown that Black children's storytelling positively predicts their literacy skills (Gardner-Neblett, Curenton, & Blitch 2017); however, the tradition of oral storytelling in many Black communities and communal spaces such as places of worship does not always use the beginning-middle-end structure common in early literacy curricula and thus is sometimes devalued by teachers (Bredekamp & Willer 2022; Delpit 1995). As you listen to children tell and retell stories, be open to more than one way of retelling and identify the strengths in children's oral language skills rather than adherence to set form.

Here are some tips for using technologies for viewing and reviewing:

> **Make a class book together.** Children can learn the process of using the app by making a book. This project also includes modeling for oral language because children can listen to what their teachers and peers say.

> **Start with guided practice.** Children need support in learning how to operate an app independently as well as in thinking about what to say. During guided practice, prompting and questions are key scaffolds.

> **Expect background noise.** When teachers record a class book, the background noise can be minimized, but if children are working independently, the recording feature will pick up the noises of a busy classroom. Teach children how to speak loud enough so that background noise is not an issue. Also, think about where in the room children should record, perhaps creating a "recording studio," which could be a large cardboard box with pillows inside to mute the background noise (purchasing a microphone attachment can also help). However, building a space like this might cancel out the value of a tablet being more portable for view-and-review activities. In that case, think about where the children are likely to sit to record and locate that area away from the noisier play areas.

> **Plan a variety of whole class, small group, and independent projects.** Consider your objectives for a project and whether these are best served by children working with others or trying to come up with their own ideas and language. Individual children may respond differently in different settings; some children thrive speaking in front of their peers and others prefer to record in smaller groups or one-on-one with a teacher. Further, some children will be familiar with technologies because they have the same resources at home, and some may only have opportunities to use these technologies at school. Consider the individuals in your classroom and provide differentiated support and opportunities to best fit their needs.

> **Have children share.** Children are motivated to share their work with their peers, but sharing is also motivating for the audience. Hearing from peers is inspiring, and children learn new ideas they might want to try by asking questions about process.

Storytelling

"We are, as a species, addicted to story. Even when the body goes to sleep, the mind stays up all night, telling itself stories" (Gottschall 2012, xiv). Young children love to tell adults about their days, their families, and fantastical stories from their imaginations. Using technologies to capture children's stories is a powerful way to integrate digital tools into the classroom. Recording stories can be done simply. Similar to a view-and-review activity, children can take a photo of a drawing or other artwork and tell a story over it. Two other processes for bringing children's stories to life are story acting and movie making.

Story Acting

More than 40 years ago, Vivian Gussin Paley (1981) introduced early childhood educators to story acting as a way to support and extend the drama, creativity, and problem solving that she saw children engaging in during play. She would invite children to each dictate a story, which was often based in their play interests, and later involve the whole class in acting out each of these stories. This technique lets the teacher ask a child questions to further the story and encourages the child to experience and puzzle through all of the thoughts and feelings they are expressing in their stories. Adding technologies, and the new role that comes with them, can refresh this time-honored practice.

What Does Story Acting Look Like?

Story acting starts with story dictation. A teacher meets with a child one-on-one and asks the child to tell a story by using a phrase such as "Tell me your story" or "How does your story begin?" The teacher then writes the child's story word for word. To honor the child's thoughts and to create a time capsule of this point in the child's development, grammar is not corrected. If the child pauses or tells a very brief story, the teacher can ask questions to help them extend the story or to tease out details of the story (see "Story Starters" on page 60). Once the child indicates that the story is complete, the teacher reads the story back to the child and asks which role they would like to play when the group acts it out.

At large group time, the teacher reads aloud that child's story and works with the children to assign roles. Children can accept or pass on any role. Roles include all the characters and key objects in the story. Using technologies includes an additional role: the child acting as videographer, holding the camera to record the story. Children who are not playing a role are the audience. Once all roles are assigned and the children are ready, the videographer begins recording, the teacher reads the story aloud again, and the children act out their roles in the story. The teacher announces, "the end," the audience claps, and the videographer stops recording.

Video-recording the story acting with a camera app and sharing it in a digital portfolio adds two new facets to this time-honored approach: more child direction and a wider audience. Story acting is child centered—children are both authors of and actors in the story—so a child is also the videographer. The teacher gives minimal direction to the videographer, prompting the child to make sure they can see all the actors in the story and giving cues to start and stop recording. The child holds the device, moves it to get the right opening view or to capture new action in the story, and presses the button to start and stop the filming. Controlling the device gives children agency as creators and helps them learn how to maneuver the technology to get the results they want.

If a child is reluctant to act out a story in front of a group, suggest the role of videographer as another way to participate in story acting. Some children initially turn down the opportunity to tell stories because they don't want to act and do not see another way to participate. When offered the chance to tell their story and take the role of videographer, initially reluctant storytellers often begin to tell and record their own stories, and some eventually act in them.

The story-acting sessions can also be shared, which can be motivating for some children who like to know that others will be able to see their stories. Teachers can play story-acting videos for the class and share with families via blogs or digital portfolios. Families can also be invited to story-act with their children at home and send a video to the class. Story acting at home is an opportunity to draw on familial funds of knowledge; oral storytelling is a common heritage practice and gives families the opportunity to share some of their culture with the class. Further, when the curriculum builds on assets from home, children connect more readily with classroom learning and are more likely to feel a sense of belonging (Iruka 2022).

Here are some tips for using technologies during story acting:

> **Repeat the story to make sure you get all the words.** Read the child's words aloud as you write them to keep pace with the storyteller.

> **Get many children involved.** Large objects such as houses, castles, and trees can also be characters, sometimes incorporating multiple children working together. For example, several children could hold hands in a circle to be the pot that a character is stirring.

> **Keep the story-acting sessions short and frequent.** Children need to learn how to be a good audience, but if you ask them to sit for too long, they will lose attention and perhaps enthusiasm for the stories being acted out.

> **Keep track of who has told a story.** Some children are eager storytellers, and some need encouragement. Use craft sticks with the children's names on them to randomly choose volunteers for actors or videographers. This also assures children who did not have a chance to act in one story that they will have a turn the next time. Children should have the opportunity to turn down acting in a story.

> **Story acting is about the children.** They should be the storytellers, actors, scenery makers, and videographers.

Story Starters

Use these questions and phrases to extend a child's story when beginning a story-acting session:

> Tell me about your story.

> How does your story begin?

> Who is in your story?

> What happens next?

> What is (your character) going to do now?

> How does (that character) feel about that?

> Where are (your characters)?

> What happens when . . . ?

> Is there anything else that happens?

> How does your story end?

> **Emphasize process, not perfection.** Using technologies to video-record may provide motivation and a wider audience, but it can also cause teachers to feel like it should be perfect. Instead, focus on what the children are learning from fully engaging in all parts of the story acting.

Movie Making

One way my family and I filled our extra time during the COVID-19 pandemic was by making short movies. We recorded a music video for a song that my sons and husband wrote about the virus and recorded a choreographed Star-Wars-esque light-saber duel. For each video, we discussed the story we wanted to tell, the shots we needed to record, and the angles that worked best for a particular shot. Using movie editing software, my 8- and 12-year-old sons knit together the scenes, overlaid sound effects and music, and added visual effects to make it look as if we were holding real light sabers.

Advancements in digital tools have made it possible for my sons to do all this at home with their own creative energy, critical thinking, problem solving, and perseverance. They are motivated to finish a project because they want to tell stories and share them with their friends and family. My sons' editing skills have developed far beyond what they could do when they first started making simpler movies at a younger age. Using apps that offer more scaffolding, they first learned the foundational skills of movie making, such as how to make a story with a beginning, middle, and end; how to collaborate with others on a storyline; how to position a camera to get a shot; and how to convey emotion through music. Apps for digital puppetry, stop-motion movies, and movie trailers all provide scaffolding and are available on tablets and similar devices.

Digital Puppetry

With digital puppet apps, children choose puppets and backgrounds and then record audio and video while acting with digital puppets as if they were tangible puppets. Children may use a selection of stock characters and backgrounds or use photos to put real faces on the puppets and design their own backgrounds. With the latter feature, children tell inclusive stories that reflect the diversity of their friends as characters or expand the diversity by adding faces from famous individuals or story characters from many cultures. Digital puppet apps help children develop the foundational storytelling ideas of characters, setting, and plot while making movies without having to edit.

Digital puppet shows can also be used as alternative forms of nonfiction presentations. One second grade teacher had her students use a puppet app for their presentations on famous Americans. They could choose puppets to represent the person who was the subject of their presentation or create a puppet to represent the person more accurately. The students researched their subjects and wrote short speeches to record while their puppets moved along the background they created. Some children included more than one puppet to represent other people in their subject's life.

Stop-Motion

Young children can make stop-motion movies by using toys or familiar objects to tell a story. Moving toys around to tell a story is something children do all the time in play, so stop-motion movies feel familiar to them. Because the children must take a picture after each movement of a character to complete the film, they practice patience and concentration. However, stop-motion movie making is also relatively forgiving. Adults may be familiar with clay animation as a form of stop-motion movie making in which animators use hundreds of shots for just a few seconds of professional film. However, stop-motion movies can be made with much fewer shots and still result in a satisfactory movie, making this type of app accessible to young children.

Movie Trailer Templates

Some movie-editing software has templates for a movie trailer, complete with music that reflects a particular genre (such as adventure or comedy), slides for adding text, and places to drop in short videos. These templates provide scaffolding for young movie makers with suggestions for scenes (action shot, wide shot, etc.) and background music to suggest a mood. Children also don't have to learn how to edit the length of a video or even consider how long they want to shoot a scene; they can just drop it into the template and the presets will adjust it for them. In addition, if children want to use still photos, the template has presets that will pan across the photo to give it movement. That said, this type of app is the most complicated of the three suggestions in this section, and children will need modeling and guided practice before they work independently. Movie trailer templates might be more appropriate for children in second or third grade, where children can use them to retell or create new stories or as an alternative to more traditional assignments. For example, rather than write a report about an endangered species, second graders could make a trailer with pictures or video with information about the animal and ways to help save it. Making a movie trailer is also a great project for multiage groups of children because younger children can help create a storyline and act while older children use the app to edit the video.

Here are some tips for making movies:

> **Talk with children about their ideas.** Children need support in developing a plan for a story before they begin using an app. They can use storyboarding to plan out the story in pictures or talk to a teacher about their ideas. It's much easier for children to collaborate when they all agree on their story beforehand. They don't need a script or a complete narrative, just general ideas and a plan to guide their work in the context of that story.

> **Support children's understanding and use of storytelling by reading or telling stories frequently.** Folktales and fairy tales have clear characters, setting, and plots that children can build on. Include a variety of stories from many cultures, such as *Lon Po Po* (a Chinese tale), *Anansi the Spider* (a West African tale), and *The Talking Eggs* (adapted from a Creole tale). Consider inclusive retellings of European fairy tales such as *La Princesa and the Pea* by Susan Middleton Elya, a bilingual Spanish-English retelling with illustrations by Juana Martinez-Neal that features textiles inspired by indigenous peoples of Peru, or illustrator Rachel Isadora's retelling of *Rapunzel* in an African setting.

> **Encourage mixing of media.** The first movie trailer my son made was based on *Star Wars*. He loved the storytelling in that series and was motivated to make his own version. Borrowing characters from popular media is similar to borrowing a character from a fairytale. As young children begin telling stories, using familiar characters can provide scaffolding as they come up with their own plot. (See "Making Intentional Choices" on page 67.)

> **Consider small group projects.** All of these movie-making processes can be done by one person, but many apps also have great potential for collaborative work. Collaborative storytelling pushes creation beyond simply learning to tell a story and supports children in learning social and emotional skills. To make a successful story together, children have to communicate clearly, listen to each other, negotiate, and use impulse control and problem-solving skills.

> **Emphasize the process of creating rather than the finished product.** Have developmentally appropriate expectations for the products and storytelling that young children will be able to produce—their skill in using the apps will increase over time. When my son first started making stop-motion movies at age 5, you could often see his sneakers in the edge of the frame. I pointed this out to him, and over time he gained enough control of the camera and the story to fix this. But from the beginning, I both provided feedback and celebrated his accomplishment of making a short story with stop-motion. Apps will almost always have more functionality than the children can realistically take advantage of; the child's individual abilities, not the app's capabilities, should determine the objectives. Focus on the enjoyment, excitement, and challenge that the continual learning process brings.

Coding

To a layperson, writing lines of code may not seem similar to other creative acts such as storytelling or making art. Coding, however, is a type of making. In the same way that a child might create a plan for building a city and then construct it, a child coding the path of a robot must create a plan for movement and then execute it. Writing lines of code is complex and beyond the abilities of young children; however, there are apps or toys that allow children to practice coding in a developmentally appropriate way.

Coding runs many of the tools used in daily life, from the simple program that turns on a light when opening a refrigerator door to the complex storytelling and functions within computer games. Essentially, coding is creating a sequence of instructions. Advanced coders choose a specific coding language to accomplish this, but developers have created toys and apps that allow children to learn about coding in a developmentally appropriate way through building with tangible objects or sequencing simple icons. In addition, McLennan (2017) suggests pre-coding games in which children direct a classmate through a grid (drawn or taped to the floor) by giving a sequence of directions (e.g., take one step forward, turn right, take two steps forward). These kinds of games allow children to practice some coding skills without needing access to any digital tools.

Until recently, coding instruction was focused on older children, but a large study by Bers, González-González, and Armas-Torres (2019) found that even 3-year-olds enjoyed and could program a robot designed to support children in learning to code. Coding aligns well with the play mindset, as children go through a creative and problem-solving cycle, often collaboratively:

1. Decide on a task to complete (for example, getting the robot to turn in a circle).

2. Design the code or sequence of directions.

3. Test the code by running it.

4. Evaluate whether or not the task was completed.

5. Refine the code as needed.

6. Test again.

As with other technologies, it is critical to focus on the process rather than the product or outcome to highlight the learning and thinking children engage in when faced with failed codes and the need to make refinements. Perhaps differently than some other forms of play, children do best when they have an objective for coding (Bers, González-González, & Armas-Torres 2019). Physical tools used in coding for young children often resemble blocks, so without a goal for coding, children may simply build with the blocks rather than code. McLennan (2017) suggests using a goal of retelling familiar stories; children in her program use coding to move through a story setting and think about order. For example, the gingerbread man must move two spaces up to the cow, and then turn and move two spaces to the pig, and so on to go through retelling the whole story. With a goal to get a robot or character to accomplish something, children will actively engage in problem-solving cycles and even come up with their own goals.

Several coding apps available present goals for a child, such as the LEGO MINDSTORMS app in which children enter a sequence of instructions to move a robot through a factory. There are also more open-ended coding technologies, like Osmo coding kits, in which a child enters a sequence of instructions to control a character's movement through a world, and Scratch Junior, in which children make a video game, including drawing the characters. Some children associate coding with computer games, which may make coding attractive to them. In addition, coding programs like Scratch Junior also give children the option to share what they have made with other coders.

Coding in an app can be a challenge for young children because the process is more abstract and may require reading ability to choose a command for a sequence. Coding robots can be a better place to start because they offer a tactile experience. Children use either buttons or a remote to enter a sequence of movements (move forward, turn, move backward) that the robot then performs. Entering this sequence requires a goal and planning. Taping a grid on the floor can give children a visual aid in planning out what sequence of movements they will need to accomplish their goal. Children can even pretend to be the robot and step through the grid to figure out which movements they need to enter. Some coding robots also come with large cards that the children can lay out to help plan the sequence of instructions they will give the robot. Visual cues such as a grid or coding cards can support young children in remembering the sequence. If the sequence does not accomplish the goal, they can go back to the instructions to figure out what they need to change.

Here are some tips for using a coding robot:

> **Introduce simple tasks to help children learn about a sequence of directions.** Start with the challenge of getting the robot to move straight, then add turns, and then move on to more complicated sequences.

> **Provide a way for children to track directions.** Apps and some robots will come with a method for tracking directions that the user has already input. If this method is not provided, draw arrows on index cards.

> **Model problem solving.** Use phrases such as, "Hmm, your character or robot didn't do what you expected. What can you try?" In coding, it's just as important to identify what you did correctly as it is to examine a mistake, learn from it, and revise.

> **Teach coding skills independent from a robot or app.** As mentioned previously, McLennan (2017) uses a grid taped to the floor or drawn with chalk on the ground as the basis for a coding sequence. Children take turns giving each other directions similar to those used for coding a robot or in an app (move one space forward, turn to the left, move one space forward).

Assessment

Each creative act in this chapter is an opportunity for teachers to learn more about the children they work with. Using technologies for assessment is not new, but it has often been limited to using software or websites for data entry or analyzing benchmark assessments. DAP promotes the use of a variety of assessment types, such as portfolios and notes based on observations of children (Scott-Little, with Reschke 2022). Similar to a print portfolio, digital portfolios allow teachers to assess growth over time while adding capabilities such as using video and audio to directly assess oral language development. Teachers can also share digital portfolios to keep families informed about their children's progress regularly. In addition, using technologies for assessment can help teachers transition their focus away from the product in favor of the process (Danniels, Pyle, & DeLuca 2020). Further, including children's creative acts in the assessment process supports culturally sustaining pedagogy (Ladson-Billings 2014; Paris & Alim 2014); open-ended assignments allow children to draw on their own funds of knowledge to shape the final product. This helps children feel included and valued by the school and program community. No matter the type of assessment used, it should be aligned with objectives appropriate to the children's developmental levels and needs (Scott-Little, with Reschke 2022).

Portfolios

The creative acts discussed in this chapter will all result in a digital product. These products can be valuable contributions to a portfolio, documenting a child's learning over time. With digital portfolio apps, a teacher uploads a child's digital product and then tags the product with one or more labels. With these labels, the teacher can sort a portfolio in a variety of ways—for example, the teacher can look at a child's work sample from early in the year and compare it with a product from the end of the year to see growth over time. This can be particularly helpful in reviewing oral language goals. Comparing Arjun's products from October with those created in June, his teachers could easily see the remarkable change in his English vocabulary (see Chapter 4). A teacher can also label products by topic or type of activity to see growth over time in particular areas. Finally, teachers can choose to share these portfolios with families. Sharing allows families to see their child's progress all year long from regular digital work samples rather than just at family–teacher conferences (see Chapter 6).

Assessing Process

When using technologies as assessments, as in other forms of learning, it is important that teachers use observation to assess the learning that happens during the creative process, which often is not captured in the final project. Teachers can observe children using technology and take anecdotal notes to capture the knowledge demonstrated in the process. For example, when I watched preschooler Georgia use an app to record a story over a picture she drew, I learned a lot about what she knew about technology, storytelling, and print and took notes on all of it. She recalled all the steps to complete the process: opening the storytelling app, selecting a photo, starting a voice recording, and stopping the recording. She understood environmental print, selecting the correct icon to open the camera app to take a picture and then selecting another icon to switch apps so that she could do the recording. I noticed that she still needed a prompt to hold the tablet correctly, but after I said, "Will you see your whole drawing in that picture?" she corrected her positioning. Her story was, as it had been several times before, about her parents, which prompted me to think of ways to encourage her to tell stories about a variety of topics. Finally, she could independently use the text feature in the app to write her name over the photo, but I noticed that she asked me to help her write "love." She could, however, find the letters on the keyboard, and when she pressed v, she said to me, "That's like V, like your name." My observations of Georgia's process of creating a product with technologies helped me assess many areas of her learning.

Finally, using creative acts as assessments of children's learning allows for more culturally sustaining practices by positioning children as knowledge producers, thus acknowledging their place in and value to the program community (Ladson-Billings 2014). Creating is an open-ended assignment that allows for more than one way to demonstrate competency on an assessment. Because of this open-endedness, children can make more choices and draw from their funds of knowledge, or their heritage or community practices, to express what they know (Paris & Alim 2014). However, as part of culturally sustaining practices, the teacher must also reflect on their own cultural assumptions of what should be encouraged in the classroom. See "Making Intentional Choices" for guidance in offering choices for creative acts that will reflect children's identities and support them in representing their knowledge and interests.

Next Steps

1. **Identify a creative project.** View-and-review projects can be an easy place to start.

2. **Use an app that will support the project.** Explore the app on your own before trying it with children. A variety of apps are available for supporting children in creating; you may need to try several to find one you like.

3. **Decide if you will start with a project for the entire group, a small group, or individual children.** Consider the project you have chosen, the technology you have available, and the needs and interests of the children, and choose the approach that will best fit your situation.

4. **Plan for assessment.** Will you use a digital portfolio to store or share the product? What opportunities will you have to observe the process?

MAKING INTENTIONAL CHOICES

Many Pathways for Creating

Creating with technologies opens up many possibilities for children to express their learning. It places children's knowledge at the center of learning because they are the creators. This can be empowering for many children as long as the teacher truly sees children through a strengths-based lens. This may mean accepting and supporting means of expression that are different from the ways the teacher currently expresses themselves or how they expressed themselves as children. When planning creative acts, be sure to allow for many means of expression. Here are some examples.

References to popular media elements in storytelling and play

Teachers sometimes have concerns about allowing popular media toys or themes in the program because they are concerned about violent themes, storylines that represent sexist or problematic gender representation, or repetitive play themes (Thiel 2014). However, when teachers exclude popular media references or toys in favor of open-ended toys made from nonplastic materials, this also excludes the kinds of play many children engage in in their homes and communities (Marsh 2014; Seiter 1993; Wohlwend 2017). In addition, Galbraith (2011) and Wohlwend (2017) found that allowing for the inclusion of popular media in play supported some children who did not normally join in a play group, because they were able to draw from the same fund of popular media knowledge as the other children. When teachers choose to invite popular media into creative acts, they are also inviting children to collaborate on shared interests. Mediating play with popular media characters can also create opportunities for teachers to empower children to revise problematic storylines; for example, a group of preschoolers revised princess narratives in their play to emphasize female friendship or mother–daughter relationships rather than falling in love with a prince (Wohlwend 2017).

Multimodal expression

Technologies allow for a multimodal communication. For example, children can mix print, speech, and pictures or mix video and music in movie trailers. Teachers can also encourage other modalities such as singing, rapping, spoken word poetry, or dancing to demonstrate understanding and share talents or heritage practices with teachers and friends.

Multilingual or translingual expression

Technologies that offer the option to speak or write can support dual language learners with developing English. However, they also support children's home languages and allow for translingualing, which is the mixing of languages to form new meanings. Translingualing may be as simple as using a few words from a home language mixed with English, such as a child who speaks Spanish at home saying, "Mis abuela y tías came for dinner" as they share something about their family, or as complex as texting with a mix of languages, slang, and emoji. Encouraging translingualing in creative acts can help multilingual children feel more included in a predominantly English-speaking program. "Their own day-to-day languaging practices can function as composing resources; with such a perspective, they may ultimately perceive their languages as complementary rather than interfering" (Zapata & Laman 2016, 367). Inviting and accepting children's work in a variety of languages helps sustain an inclusive environment.

CHAPTER 6

A Connected Classroom

> Dropping Arjun off at school is difficult for his mom. Arjun cries and holds on to her, as do many preschoolers who are struggling with the transition from home to program, but his feelings are also influenced by the fact that he is a dual language learner. Arjun's bilingual parents and his grandparents speak Gujarati at home with Arjun so that he will have a firm foundation in this language before hearing and speaking English all day in school and in town.
>
> Arjun's school uses a digital portfolio for each student, so after a tearful drop-off, Arjun's mother can go online and see pictures of him playing on the playground (sometime minutes later) and hear a recording of his emerging English skills as he talks about his thoughts overlaying a picture he drew. Years later, his mother would still remember the "All About Me" interview Arjun records with his teacher, Miss Christi, his first October in the program. When Miss Christi asks, "How do you feel at school?" Arjun whispers, "Happy."

What does it mean to be connected? In the digital age, this might engender some anxiety as many people feel *too* connected. Video conferencing, email, and file sharing all mean that work can be done or continued at home. Smartphones make some people feel they have to be available to everyone all the time. So much connectivity can make people want to go off the grid or unplug. However, technologies have also made life easier: people can easily talk to loved ones across the country or even across the globe, and some enjoy the flexibility of working from home.

I joined social media because of my family. When my first son was born, my sister, whom I am very close to, and I lived on opposite coasts of the country, and she could fly to see us only a few times a year. But she could watch her nephew grow up via videos and pictures I posted on social media, even though she was miles away and in a different time zone. My sister and I now live on the same coast but still not in the same state, so my two sons regularly see, interact with, and build a relationship with her toddler son using video chat.

This connectivity is powerful, but it is nurtured by visiting each other often. The cousins have built a powerful family bond from in-person experiences, and technologies help fill in the gaps. My sons are excited when the video chat rings or when my sister posts a video of her son to social media. These moments give us a peek into their cousin's daily life. It's this kind of positive relational connectivity that educators can harness to strengthen their school and program communities.

School can feel like a mystery to some families. They have a vague idea of what goes on from their own experiences and school communications, but children spend hours at school. They enter the program in the morning and come home in the afternoon, and what happens in the middle seems a big blank to many families. If you ask children what they did at school that day, they often don't give much of an answer. The school day is long for young children, and it can be difficult for them to sort through the many events of the day and figure out what is significant. If I can ask my children about something specific ("Tell me about your wind experiment" or "How was your clay sculpture project in art?"), they give more detailed stories because the questions help them sift through the day and focus on one aspect of the events. However, I don't always know specifics to ask about. Teachers can demystify the school day by creating respectful, reciprocal partnerships with families through regular communication and invitations for families to participate as well as share needs, preferences, and question (Mancilla & Blanco 2022; NAEYC 2020).

Creating a Connected Classroom

Educators commonly send home weekly emails with the topics taught, books read, and reminders of upcoming events. Many teachers of infants and toddlers send detailed daily notes on foods eaten, diapers changed, and naps taken. These keep families informed but not necessarily connected to their child's teacher or the child's daily experiences and learning in the program. Photos are one tool for sparking a conversation between families and their children, and they can mimic the daily literacy practices many families already participate in (Marsh et al. 2017). Children regularly see family members take pictures of daily experiences and share them via text or social media. New technologies allow teachers to regularly share images, as well as videos, e-books, and other work samples, with families, creating many opportunities for windows into the classroom. Three popular ways to share these media are

> Digital portfolios, which are private with structures that mimic social media

> Virtual bulletin boards, which allow invited users to post comments or media on a shared site

> Class blogs, which combine a narrative of class events with images and sometimes links to other webpages

Teachers can use each tool to regularly share what is going on in the program. Table 3 compares the features of each tool.

Choosing a method for connecting with families is the first step but not the last or most important. Digital tools for sharing need to be used thoughtfully to strengthen the program community. The existence of a classroom blog or digital portfolio is not enough—if it is not updated regularly or families find it cumbersome to use, it will not connect families to the classroom or support conversations at home. Here are some suggestions for setting up a successfully connected classroom.

> **Choose a method and stick with it.** Routines are important for children and families. Consistently using one method helps families know what to expect and understand how to participate. Families can feel more connected to and included in the program when they know that updates are part of the routine. Before you embark on a method for sharing children's daily experiences with families, explore methods that work best for you and the children's families so that you can share on one platform and develop consistent procedures around it.

Table 3. Comparison of Connectivity Tools

	Privacy	Teacher Options	Children Can . . .	Families Can . . .
Digital portfolios	Only invited parties can see class material. Media can be tagged to be seen by the whole class, a small group, or an individual. Only those individuals tagged can view media. Families have access to their child's portfolio.	• Post pictures, videos, weblinks, and text for the whole classroom community • Post pictures, videos, weblinks, and text for individual or small groups of children • Review individual children's portfolios • Put media into folders for later review and retrieval • Control options for community interaction	• See pictures, videos, weblinks, and text posted at school and at home • Create their own work to post • Tag friends or a small group to limit sharing	• See pictures, videos, weblinks, and text posted • Be notified of a new post via their smartphone apps • See growth of their child over time • Search within their child's portfolio If option is enabled by the teacher or school: • Comment on specific pictures or media • "Like" specific pictures or media • Post family-created media • Share with other family members or friends
Blogs	Defaults to a public setting Can be set to invitation-only Anyone who has access to the blog can see each post.	• Post pictures, videos, weblinks, and text for the whole classroom community • Tag media for later review and retrieval • Control settings for community interaction	• See pictures, videos, weblinks, and text posted at school and at home • Create their own work to post	• See pictures, videos, weblinks, and text posted • Get an email notification of new posts • Share with other family members or friends If option is enabled by the teacher or school: • Comment on blog posts
Virtual bulletin boards	Defaults to a semiprivate setting Can be set to a private, password-protected, or public setting Anyone who has access to the board can see every post.	• Post pictures, videos, weblinks, and text for the whole classroom community • Can create individual boards for students or student groups • Control settings for community interaction In some versions: • Transfer posts to a portfolio student board for organization/review	• See pictures, videos, weblinks, and text posted at school and at home • Create their own work to post In some versions: • Transfer posts to a portfolio student board	• See pictures, videos, weblinks, and text posted If option is enabled by the teacher or school: • Comment on posts • Create their own posts

> **Create a plan for posting material.** Like any form of communication or record keeping, a digital communication tool is most effective when done regularly. Create a schedule for posting material, including day and time, and clarify if material is posted as part of completing a project. If children are creating and posting the materials, give them clear guidelines. Some teachers designate "documenter" as a rotating classroom job (Danniels, Pyle, & DeLuca 2020). Documenting can be a big job, so you can also plan for support from another adult to help you document, organize, or post weekly or daily material. Elicit support from a colleague or a reliable volunteer to help you keep up with communication. Make sure to give these helpers guidelines for posting procedures as well.

> **Mix media with text.** Pictures and projects give families a better sense of what is happening in the program, but they don't necessarily view the work the same way as a teacher. Use the caption function to highlight the kind of learning a child is doing or your objectives for a project or class routine. For example, preschool teacher Christi started the year by posting pictures of class routines—children waiting for a turn or a child peeling an orange—and explaining what skills the routines would help children develop, such as social and emotional skills and inhibitory control or agency and fine motor skills. The families responded enthusiastically, saying how much the teachers' views of everyday experiences helped them understand learning in early childhood. (See the photograph and captions at right.)

Most children are able to peel their own clementine. Often, they just need an adult to start it for them. This is a great fine motor skill for them, with a delicious reward at the end. —*Teachers' note to families*

"Good to know! I have been peeling them not realizing what the kids are capable of. I will bring them next co-op day." —Alexa, parent

---

"I appreciate so much how you always help reframe learning experiences like these for our family. I have a different perspective now on how to encourage different skills thanks to the teachers! Thank you." —Emerald, parent

---

> **Share authentic learning.** Even teachers who are strong advocates for children's art and child-centered programs are tempted to post only the most polished pictures and products, especially those they share via technologies. However, these products do not really let families into their children's classrooms or give them insight into the developmentally appropriate and sometimes messy processes young children engage in as they learn and create. The danger of sharing only "perfect" pictures is that families do not learn about children as they really are, and they may develop inappropriate expectations about what children's learning really looks like. That said, not every single picture or product needs to be sent home. How do you decide? A powerful example comes from Debbie, a teacher in a preschool classroom for children with disabilities. Alex, who had expressive language delays, had just finished recording about his block structure. In the recording, he had responded to some of Debbie's prompts but not all. After they were finished, I acknowledged to Debbie that the recording didn't

have as much detail as she had hoped and asked if she still wanted to post it. She responded, "It's not a lot of talking, but that is where he is right now, so I want his family to see Alex." We should always be sharing who the children are and what they do, not a more perfect, adult version of their work.

Empowering Children

New technologies can support children's agency when children choose to share the content they create with the important people in their lives. After working particularly hard to build a tall tower with blocks, preschooler Delia tapped me on the shoulder and said, "I wanna take a picture and send it to Mommy." Her teacher used an online portfolio, and Delia knew that a picture taken in the classroom could be shared with her mom at home. In the same program, Leo wrote *Popopoppoppop* in a digital drawing app and recorded, "I wrote *Pop Pop* because I love him." He announced, "Pop Pop doesn't have an iPad, but we can text it to his phone." Children want to share their work with the ones they love, and these children had digital tools for doing so. They understood that they could share their work on their own because their teachers had demonstrated how to use the online portfolio app, using the gradual release of responsibility model (modeling, guided practice, and independent practice) to support the children (see Chapter 4).

To learn new practices and processes, young children need to have them explicitly explained, demonstrated, and repeated in authentic contexts (modeling). For example, when Debbie created a book about the class rules with her students, she ended the project by saying, "I will post this book to Seesaw so that your families can learn about the class rules. You can watch it with them later and talk to them about what we do in our classroom." Debbie did not simply assume that young children and their families would interact with her classroom's digital portfolio the way that she intended, so she made her actions and intentions for the portfolio explicit.

Children also need opportunities to practice sharing their work (guided practice). When Debbie saw that Tyree had built a long train track with an elaborate city around it, she used it as an opportunity to reinforce that the children could use a tablet to document their work.

> **Miss Debbie:** "Tyree, I notice that you have created a train track that goes into a city."
>
> **Tyree:** "Yeah, it's so big!"
>
> **Miss Debbie:** "Would you like to take a picture of it and talk about it so you can share it with Mommy and Daddy at home?"
>
> **Tyree:** "Oh yeah, they're gonna be, like, wow!"
>
> Miss Debbie finds the tablet and walks through the steps of the process with Tyree. Tyree presses the icons to record and share.

After a few times of working with Debbie, Tyree will know how to do this process on his own.

DAP involves tailoring processes to children's ages and individual developmental levels; processes will not look the same for all children or all programs (Bredekamp & Willer 2022). A preschool-age child may complete the steps and talk with their teacher about what is ready to send home (independent practice), although it may be appropriate to have adult support to post. Children in the primary grades are generally able to monitor their own work and decide when it is ready to be shared. A teacher-prepared checklist might be helpful for these children to use (see the student checklist in Appendix A, page 97). In either case, blogging and online portfolios have settings that will allow the teacher to control when an item is published for families to see. Keeping this setting on ensures that the teacher is aware of each child's progress and knows which work has been shared with families.

Empowering Families

Family–teacher conferences are powerful. They are also often short and infrequent. Condensing months of experiences, learning, and growth into a 20-minute window can be dissatisfying for both families and teachers. Using technologies to share work and daily life in the program help families feel regularly connected to their child's experiences, putting less pressure on both families and teachers at conference time. When I have surveyed families about digital portfolios, they usually report that they love having a window into their child's day and that a portfolio helps them foster communication at home. They also get a better understanding of their children as learners, as did the families in the vignettes below.

> Precious's mother takes out her phone and uses the digital portfolio app at her daughter's annual Individualized Education Program (IEP) review (a conference among family members, teachers, therapists, and others to review the progress of a child with disabilities or delays and determine educational services and supports). She has concerns about Precious's language development and uses an example from her portfolio as starting point for a discussion about her goals for the next year.
>
> . . . .
>
> Arjun's mom follows his digital portfolio closely and, as the parent of a dual language learner, is eager to hear about his progress in English. She comments on his portfolio regularly, noting, "He speaks more every day!" She also supports the English-speaking teachers by translating any Gujarati: "So great to listen to him saying so much. He also used the Gujarati word for goat (bakari) in his retelling of *The Little Red Hen*."

These families found the connection to the classroom empowering. They better understood what was going on in the classroom and, importantly, how their child was learning. Because of this connection, they could then advocate for their child in conversations with the teachers.

Encouraging families to view their child's creations alongside their child offers powerful opportunities for families to build a connection to school and communicates the importance of the role of school and learning. Here are some ways families can interact with a digital portfolio:

> Ask their child to tell them more about what is happening in a picture.

> Ask questions about a piece of work. How did they make it?

> Extend the project. Repeat a science experiment, act out a story, and draw or build at home. Provide information about any apps used in your classroom so that children can use them at home too if families choose to do so.

> Write a comment together. In many apps, families can comment on posted material or coauthor comments or questions for the class.

Finally, many apps and virtual bulletin boards allow families to post pictures or videos to share with the teacher or class. Inviting families to share can strengthen their connection with the teacher, other children, and the program because their home lives are acknowledged as important. This can be a powerful way to connect home and school, but it also might feel uncomfortable for some families. You can present sharing from home as an optional "can-do" activity rather than a required "must-do" activity.

Tools like digital portfolios can provide a jumping-off point for families to talk with their child about school.

When you offer an invitation for families to share their experiences with the program in these ways, keep in mind the individual families and community and make sure that any request you make is not burdensome. Projects can be more inclusive if they're designed around taking pictures of common objects rather than a whole house or an event (such as a summer vacation, which not all families may take). Here are some ways families might share what is going on in their lives:

> Studying letters: Invite families to share pictures of labels on food packages, toys, or other objects that have words that start with a letter the class is learning about.

> Studying patterns: Invite families to share pictures of patterns in their homes or nearby outdoor areas.

> Studying plant life: Invite families to video a plant in or near their house and identify parts such as leaves and stems. Consider the communities they live in and what plants might be commonly found in the area.

> Studying families: Invite families to share a picture of their family at a community event.

> Invite family members who cannot visit the class in person to record a video of themselves cooking a family meal or sharing a family story. Again, be respectful of and sensitive to families' preferences for sharing details of their personal lives and homes.

Teachers should also consider the access families have to technologies or the cost of technologies. In places where Wi-Fi is scarce, uploading a video can require data usage that might be costly. In addition, some families may not have easy use of a tablet or smartphone. At the beginning of the year, talk to families about the technologies they commonly use, and design alternatives to support the needs in your classroom. If you know that accessing technologies will be a burden for some families, consider the following:

Having children and families photograph natural elements in their communities is one way to extend what they are learning in the program.

> What physical projects and child work can be sent home?

> What can be shared through a phone call?

> How might families share hard copies of images, stories, or completed schoolwork?

> If broadband access is an issue, is there free Wi-Fi at the program for family use? Are there community grants available to support unlimited data plans to allow sharing from a phone? (see, for example, Rodriguez-Vazquez 2020)

> How would families like to be engaged in the program? Tell families about class events and also how they can let you know if they would like to share a skill or tradition with the children.

> What community events might the teachers attend?

Using technologies can empower parents and help support and sustain family–teacher partnerships, but this can only be done when a caring relationship, not the technologies, is at the center of your communications (Bales et al. 2020). Some teachers or administrators may not feel connected to the community because their backgrounds or identities differ greatly from those of the families in the community. Zygmunt and colleagues (2018) suggest that teachers build partnerships with community mentors to better understand the community and to mitigate biases or deficit thinking and help foster understanding and connection. Later in the chapter, I discuss strategies for bridging what is commonly called the "digital divide," but this divide cannot truly be bridged unless the bridge is founded in a reciprocal relationship.

Connecting to All Educators

The children you work with may receive support services from speech therapists, physical or occupational therapists, or a teacher who provides special education services. These supports are critical but can involve a lot of information for families to manage. Technologies such as a digital portfolio of videos or photos can help teachers and therapists communicate clearly and effectively with families. Here are some suggestions:

> **Help families understand the support their child needs.** Families may not always fully understand the goals set for their child by teachers or specialists. For example, sometimes families may not see the need for supporting social skills in play because their child plays just fine at home. A teacher might share a video of the child playing during center time so that the family can see how adults' support of their child helps the child more successfully engage with peers.

> **Demonstrate key exercises.** Video or photos can provide visual cues to support families in extending practice at home. Therapists can video-record a child or send step-by-step photographs of a therapeutic exercise.

> **Document change over time.** Teachers and therapists can document children's progress on educational goals in a digital portfolio. These help the team and family review the goals and celebrate accomplishments. When Alma, a child in Michelle's inclusive preschool classroom, was working with the physical therapist to use braces to stand on her own, her teachers took a picture to send to her mom and recorded Alma saying, "Look at my strong muscles."

> **Prepare families for discussions at conferences or annual reviews.** When a child receives special services, there is often a lot of information to review at a family–teacher conference or annual review. However, families can come to the meeting already familiar with their child's progress and challenges if teachers and therapists are regularly communicating through technologies as well as during times they see the family in person. All participants will have a shared knowledge base for a deeper, more collaborative discussion.

Bridging the Digital Divide

Ownership of personal technologies such as a smartphone is on the rise in all communities; a 2021 study of internet and American life by the Pew Research Center found that 85 percent of American adults own a smartphone (Pew Research Center 2021). However, not all families have equitable access to technologies, either to devices such as tablets or computers or to high-speed broadband internet. Even as mobile device ownership has increased, access to broadband internet has not kept pace. Lack of access can often be attributed to cost and lack of network expansion; families with incomes below $30,000 a year and those who live in rural areas report that they are dependent on their smartphones to access the internet (Pew Research Center 2021). This lack of access has contributed to what has been labeled the "digital divide" or the "homework gap" because many schools assign homework that must be completed digitally. Teachers and administrators must be aware of the accessibility gap that might exist in their communities and work to bridge this gap rather than use it as an excuse for not integrating technologies into their programs. Inequitable access to technologies can widen the opportunity gap for all children to access resources to learn and succeed in school and, later on, to gain vital career-readiness skills for a workplace that increasingly requires technological competence.

It is important to understand families' access to and preferences for technologies when you choose methods of communicating and connecting with families. These tools have the possibility of increasing connection between home and school, but establishing the connection should be designed with community access in mind. Some families may interact with many types of technologies regularly, have their smartphones with them all the time, work on computers, check and respond to email regularly throughout the day. In areas where there is limited or no access to reliable or affordable broadband internet, families may use technology infrequently and rely more on cellular technologies such as a smartphone.

These differences can impact the access families have to any digital projects their children are engaging with. For example, many digital portfolios and blogs provide email templates to send to families to connect them to their child's account. This may seem like an easy, intuitive way to connect with families. However, after working with many different communities, I have found that the families who have access to computers and broadband internet either at work, home, or both tend to use email regularly; these families tended to respond to my emailed invitations to access their child portfolio within hours or days of the invitation. In contrast, in communities where families were more likely to use a smartphone to access the internet, emails often went unanswered, and some families connected to the platform only after family–teacher conferences where a teacher demonstrated the platform in person. This failure to connect was really a failure of the schools to accurately understand families' access to technologies and the devices they use regularly. Once they did get connected to the platform used by the teacher, these families checked their child's work as often as families who used email more regularly. They simply needed more support in the initial connection phase.

Finally, some families are not comfortable with unfamiliar technologies. So although they might want to participate, the prospect of navigating a new tool can be daunting on top of other challenges they may be living with. It's important that teachers and administrators acknowledge the challenges families face and offer support. During the pandemic, preschool teacher Juana Rodriguez-Vazquez found that video calls to talk families through their initial uses of digital tools helped families feel better equipped to support their child's learning at home (Rodriguez-Vazquez 2020).

To support all families in connecting to your classroom:

> **Review your communication strategies.** Survey families about the ways they prefer to receive information—by email, print, text, phone, or video calls? You might also ask them what apps they use. For example, Zoom and WhatsApp both have video chat communications, but parents may be more fluent in the app they use regularly to communicate with those in their communities.

> **Use multiple forms of invitation.** In addition to email invitation, send paper invitations with QR codes that can be read by a smartphone. If possible, include screenshots with instructions for setting up an account.

> **Offer in-person support.** If possible, create a time that families can get in-person support to connect to their child's account. If you are inviting families to share from home, show them how to post to your digital portfolio or virtual bulletin board. Consider doing this during back-to-school night or other schoolwide community night. For example, families could learn to log in to their app and create a short message for their child as a part of back-to-school night.

> **Connect families with other sources of support.** Many apps have their own tech support or FAQ sites; make sure families are aware of these in case they have a problem. You might also search for a video tutorial to make available. Be aware whether such support is available in families' home languages.

It is not only families who may struggle with access to technologies. Not all early childhood professionals have digital resources. If you are in a program with few or no digital resources, you might consider talking with your administrators and colleagues about the uses and priorities you have for digital technologies. Certainly, there are free apps and websites that can be utilized, but before you begin searching, identify your goals for communicating with technologies and then identify your digital needs and consider what you might be able to accomplish. One of the first projects I did with teachers was in a small school that used technologies only for administrative duties. They were interested in trying to use technology to support storytelling, so the school applied for and received a small community grant to get one iPad. We used only free apps, and since there was no Wi-Fi in the classroom, we were only able to share the work the children created at the end of the day when we could access the Wi-Fi in the office. This set-up was not ideal, but it worked. The teachers found free apps that suited their needs, the children created wonderful stories, and the families were enthusiastic about connecting in new ways. The next year the school reevaluated technologies use and priorities and decided that the potential benefits of having schoolwide Wi-Fi was worth fitting that cost into the budget. Using technologies doesn't have to be a big, expensive project. You can start small, look for free resources, and make slow, intentional choices about using technologies. More discussion about planning for intentional technology use follows in the next chapter.

The challenges presented by a digital divide and concerns about privacy when using technologies (see "Making Intentional Choices" on page 81) should not deter administrators from working toward a more connected program or school. Programs implementing DAP make it a priority to form partnerships with families. Some educators I have worked with have attempted to connect with families by sending surveys or inviting them to come into the school. While these practices were helpful in some cases, they did not meet every family's needs; surveys went unanswered or families were unable or hesitant to come in during program hours (or at all). These educators felt that they had, at best, a loose connection with families. In contrast, educators who use newer technologies to connect with families tend to have stronger family–classroom connections. I can't say definitively why this is, but I think it is because the families see and hear what is going on in the classroom through the digital communications; they have a sense of their child's day, and the school feels familiar and comfortable. They are no longer looking for a window into the program—the window is already open to them.

Consider the words below from Debbie, a teacher in a classroom for preschoolers with disabilities:

> I like that (the families) see us. Miss Cynthia is known as the behavior expert in the classroom, and they love that because they see such a difference in their child's behavior, but they never got to see the silly side of her. Well, in some of these videos she is being super silly . . . so they can see that you can be silly with the kids. Or one day, we were videoing four kids interacting. Sanaa wasn't verbally interacting with the other kids, but you could see on video that they were engaging with her. She was actually making eye contact and smiling at what they were saying. But if you were to write that down on paper or just share an audio recording, you would think she wasn't participating, but she was, in her way. She was smiling and grabbing their hands. Sanaa's mom expressed that last year Sanaa didn't have any peer friendships, and this year her mom can see pictures of her interacting with her peers and even just being accepted. She got to see them playing hair salon and playing in the kitchen area. She is not just being told that Sanaa is interacting—she is seeing Sanaa's friends loving her and playing with her hair. She never had that before.

Next Steps

1. **Talk to your colleagues and administrators about how a connected classroom would work in your school.** How might families in your community respond?

2. **Explore different platforms or apps for sharing what the children are exploring and learning.** Consider the capabilities of each option and how those capabilities match your goals and resources.

3. **Create a space for connecting with families.** Set up a digital portfolio or class blog to share children's work and classroom life. Talk to children and families about how you will share their work. Be sure to follow your school's media policy.

Digital Tools for Learning, Creating, and Thinking

Privacy Considerations

Sharing pictures, videos, and projects from your classroom can help families feel more connected to the classroom, school, and even other families because they all have access to common experiences. However, it's important to share experiences appropriately in a way that doesn't violate a family's or child's privacy. There are important questions to ask about any platform before sharing materials.

Do you have permission to share?

Early childhood programs should have media policies and consent forms so that families can have a say in how images or recordings of their children are used. Make sure to review this policy with your administrators; make sure they know how something like a digital portfolio app works and discuss whether it aligns with existing policy or whether a new policy needs to be created. Make sure families are clear on what you plan to do; describe what materials you plan to post and be clear about privacy settings. Ask families to opt in rather than opt out so that they are actively making choices about how to participate. In addition, be sure to follow up in person or over the phone with any families that don't respond to make sure they have the opportunity to ask questions and do not lose out on opportunities to connect with the classroom because they did not respond to the first request.

Who can see what is posted?

Whether you are using an online digital portfolio, blog, or other sharing application, check the privacy settings. These will allow you to control who can see the children's work. Most often the options will be

> Public—material can be accessed by anyone

> Private—only you can access the material

> Permission only—you grant access to the material to specific people (families and students)

Choose a setting that allows you to connect with families without compromising their privacy. If an app will not allow you to control the privacy settings, look for another app rather than risk infringing on families' privacy.

What can viewers do with the material?

It is important to know what the platform allows viewers to do with the material you post. Can they comment on a post? Can they download it for their own use? Is there a direct link to share it on another platform like social media? These options are not always immediately obvious, so check the privacy settings on any app or platform you are thinking about so that you can make an informed decision about whether or not to use it or how to adjust the settings as appropriate for your situation. If you allow for commenting, talk to families about doing so in ways that build a supportive online community.

What does the app do with the data?

Check the privacy settings to ensure that using a service does not automatically allow a company to collect information about you and your class, as some social media sites do. The site or application should make it clear that it does not use any of the data you post. There are reputable companies working with school settings that realize the importance of protecting family privacy and will not attempt to use any of the data you post.

Finally, all of these choices must align with federal law. Photos, videos, and even work samples of children could be covered by the Family Educational Rights and Privacy Act, or FERPA; administrators and teachers should be sure that their media policy aligns with the law. For more information, visit https://studentprivacy.ed.gov.

CHAPTER 7

Planning for Intentional Technologies Integration

The technologies available in schools varies widely. I have seen schools with no technology because they have intentionally chosen to exclude it, programs that have just a few devices, those with many devices, and programs that do not have the budget to purchase technologies. I know teachers who have written grants to get just one tablet when they had none, schools that worked with families to raise money to purchase technologies, and also schools that had large budgets and numerous name-brand tablets that were rarely touched because the teachers did not see how to fit them into the curriculum. The presence of technologies in the classroom is not a guarantee of effective use, if used at all (Blackwell 2013). It's critical to plan for the intentional use of a technology before it's purchased, including setting goals, deciding how and when it will be used, and identifying key partners for success. Planning is not just for those who are fortunate enough to have a budget that allows for them to identify any tool and purchase it. When you identify your goals, you may see that existing resources can be used to achieve those goals. Further, if new technologies are what you need, planning can help you identify what you might be able to get for free and what needs to be purchased. You can then work with your program to set priorities, reallocate budgets if necessary, fundraise, or apply for funds through a grant. Once your purpose is clear, you can review your situation and intentionally acquire or repurpose tools that will set you up for successful, sustained technology use.

Setting a Purpose

In 2005, my first year of teaching kindergarten, our school purchased an interactive whiteboard. I was fascinated by the device. It wasn't just that it was new or that its newness piqued the children's interest. In fact, at the time, I had to sign out the one board available, drag it down three hallways, and set it up—these hurdles quickly spoiled some of its newness. I was fascinated with it was because it helped me reach my teaching objectives in new ways.

With the interactive whiteboard, I could write down ideas as the children in my class called them out, and then we could step back and look at our ideas to sort them. Unlike shared writing on chart paper, I could move words across the board with a drag of my fingers, creating new categories. For example, when we did a study of frogs, I probed the children's prior knowledge by asking them to call out anything they knew about frogs. Their responses included, "They can jump," "They go in water," "I saw one in a pond," and "They eat flies." We started swiping these ideas into categories—habitat, food, abilities—to see what we knew and what questions we had.

Later, when we watched a video about frogs on the whiteboard, we could pause and use the smart pen to draw on the video, highlighting what we noticed. The interactive whiteboard enabled me to support the children's thinking, encourage them to reflect on their ideas, add to their ideas, and use their powers of observation to gain new knowledge. Many years later, the interactive whiteboard I used is outdated, but the idea that technology is a tool that teachers can use intentionally to improve instruction is not.

Setting Goals

In some classrooms, technologies are not used as tools but rather as the end in itself—a tablet that's used rarely and randomly or a computer center with a set of websites or apps that, while vaguely aligned with class topics and evaluated for age appropriateness, the children use only during free or center time. Mertala (2017) notes that when teachers relegate technology use to limited times, the apps they use tend to be close ended and sometimes at odds with the child-centered teaching beliefs these teachers hold. The purpose for technologies during free time or in computer centers often seems to be ill defined. At best, some of the children will practice some skills and work on taking turns; at worst, the children are just being occupied with technology and, in some cases, fighting over it. Technology in these situations is not used intentionally or in developmentally appropriate ways. As informed and intentional decision makers, teachers must have goals for their technology tools.

Some teachers who are familiar with setting goals and objectives for learning in content areas may be mystified about doing so for technologies. Wiggins and McTighe (2005) champion the idea of backwards design: teachers start with the goal they have for learning and then decide what learning activity will help children reach this goal or understanding. Contrast this to starting with an activity that sounds fun and then trying to figure out what the children learned at the end of it, which makes the activity the goal itself rather than a medium for learning. (This is not the same as emergent curriculum, in which teachers consider the learning that may occur as they create learning opportunities based on careful observation of children's interests, ideas, and questions [Masterson 2022].) As discussed in Chapter 4, teachers do need to provide instruction on how to use new technologies; however, learning to use technologies should not be the main objective. Technologies should support existing learning goals, and considering how children might create, collaborate, or communicate with technologies (see Chapter 2) is a good starting point.

Create

As discussed in previous chapters, there are two different approaches for using technologies as creative tools:

1. How can educators support children in reflecting on the process of creating by using technologies?

2. How can children use technologies to create something new?

Creating takes many forms, such as collage making, painting, building with blocks, making complex train tracks with stops at houses and fire stations, using loose parts to make a simple machine, and creating props for dramatic play. Using technologies to capture a child's work and then encouraging that child to reflect on the work supports several goals, including

> Supporting the development of linear thought processes as children recount first, next, and last steps

> Developing descriptive vocabulary

> Applying new vocabulary from a unit of study

Technologies can also be used to create. New technologies offer powerful storytelling tools to record stories, write books, create puppet shows, or make movies. These creative acts meet goals such as

> Developing comprehension skills

> Developing descriptive vocabulary (e.g., *gigantic*, *terrifying*) or academic vocabulary (*migration*, *reptile*, *molting*) through describing what they see in a picture

> Counting and categorizing

> Supporting understanding through acting

> Revising a project

> Developing executive functioning

> Developing a growth (or maker) mindset

> Persevering to finish a project

> Developing social and emotional skills by collaborating on a project or building empathy through storytelling

Collaborate

Working with someone else can be challenging, even for adults! Learning to collaborate is a broad goal that will support children for school success and beyond. But what does it mean to collaborate? To support children in developing these critical social and emotional skills, educators must teach these skills just as they would any other in the curriculum. Identifying goals for collaboration and the collaborative skills children need to develop can help teachers intentionally plan opportunities for learning. Certainly, some of these lessons will take place without technologies, but teachers can also set collaboration goals for technology with projects that encourage children to collaborate to be successful. For example, when children use a digital puppet show app, listening might be a goal; it's hard to co-construct a story if you don't listen to your partner (although some children might try!). Teachers can actively teach about listening as well as observe and support partners during a project. Collaboration goals might include

> Listening

> Taking turns

> Questioning

> Communicating needs

> Making compromises

> Building empathy

Collaboration doesn't just have to be between children; teachers can partner with children on projects. Just as children come to early childhood programs with different development levels in academic and language skills, they also have varying social and emotional skills. For some children, collaborating with a teacher can provide the scaffolding they need as they are practicing critical collaboration skills.

Communicate

Children build communication skills as they use technologies to create and collaborate with partners. For planning purposes, think about the communication needed between teachers and families. As discussed in Chapter 6, technologies offer a powerful tool to connect families to their child's program. Even just using technologies to share images of what's going on in the program has helped families feel more connected. However, intentionally planning for this sharing can increase the feeling of connection and make technologies more powerful communication tools.

Adding captions under projects that children have created or photos of a class activity can help draw families' attention to a skill that is being developed or practiced. Here are some examples:

> Under a photo of a preschooler's writing sample, explain developmental understandings of writing with the caption "Young children are just starting to figure out how to use letters to communicate through writing. When your child is writing, encourage them to stretch out the word they want to write and listen for letters they know. At first your child might not identify all the sounds or letters in a word. That is okay. Encourage them to write the letters they hear."

> Under a picture of a first grader independently reading, acknowledge their accomplishments: "Ang has really enjoyed our new book corner. His ability to focus and read on his own has really improved since the beginning of the year. Today he finished Dav Pilkey's *A Friend for Dragon* and really enjoyed it. You can ask him about it at home."

> Under a picture of kindergartners on a nature walk, explain the related science concepts and vocabulary: "We went on a walk outside today to classify trees. The children looked for deciduous trees (those that lose their leaves in winter) and evergreen trees (those with needles that stay green all year). Classifying is an important scientific skill. You and your child can look to see what kinds of trees are around your home!"

> Under videos created with a drawing app during a kindergarten study of addition, you can explain, "Drawing can help children understand what is being represented in a number sentence. Right now, the children are counting objects to figure out the answer, but over the year they will build their math memory so that they know the sum without counting."

As you intentionally plan what you want to communicate with families and why, consider how, for example, pictures of particular class activities or routines can illuminate the program community or individual child accomplishments and highlight aspects of development.

Classroom Activities

Teachers intentionally choose daily activities to support children's social, emotional, and fine motor skills and content learning. You can communicate to families what their children are learning by, for example, adding a caption to a photo of children during morning meeting that explains how this routine helps children practice inhibitory control as they wait for their turn to speak and supports a sense of belonging and emotional awareness. Some other messages around activity goals might be

> How class routines support child development (executive functioning, social emotional skills, fine or gross motor skills)

> How class routines and small group experiences support emergent literacy and numeracy

> How exploration at center time helps support emergent math concepts (e.g., measuring tall towers in the block center or making patterns in the art center) or emergent literacy (e.g., writing menus and customer orders while playing restaurant in the dramatic play center)

> How children work with partners to develop their skills (e.g., reading with a buddy during literacy or solving a math problem together)

> How class visitors or field trips support content knowledge (e.g., "Ask your child what the dentist taught us about keeping our teeth clean!" Or "This is an albino snake from the zoo—'albino' is a big new vocabulary word the zookeeper taught us. Ask your child about the challenges albino animals have!")

Individual Child Accomplishments

Teachers are observing and noticing children changing and growing in small and big ways all the time. For example, preschool teacher Anneliese knows that Jake is improving in his ability to focus on a project and persevere at it. Out on the playground, she sees that Jake and Aditi are investigating the large chunk of ice in the corner. She notices their curiosity about what is underneath the ice and how they might move it, their persistence and cognitive flexibility in trying different tools to lift or break the ice, and their pride when they finally accomplish their goal. A picture of this wouldn't fully communicate what Anneliese sees, but the caption that she writes underneath the picture to share with families does.

In terms of planning and goal setting, you can plan for assessment documentation in two ways. One way is to ask yourself where you have observed a child starting to demonstrate growth or whether a family has expressed a concern about an area of their child's development (for example, friendships or writing their name). You can be on the lookout to document a child's growth and work in these areas. A second way is to assign yourself, or your team, children to focus your observations on for the day or week and to document their learning. Either way you plan, use a system to track your observations so that you can be intentional about communicating your findings with all families. Especially when sharing pictures, some children will tend to jump in front of the camera or be eager to create something, and some will shy away. You don't need an equal number of pictures or work examples for each child, but you should make sure that every family hears about their child regularly. The weekly planning sheet in Appendix B on page 98 has a section labeled "Focus children" to give you a space to plan for this weekly and to keep track of the children you have observed so you can ensure that every child is a focus child many times throughout the year.

Some areas of development to consider for communication with families are

> Language development

> Reaching a goal

> Growth in social relationships

> Focus or persistence

> Curiosity

> New cognitive skills

Teachers can never plan for everything that will happen, but if you view technologies as tools for communicating with families, you might be a little more ready to capture a learning moment or accomplishment when it occurs. As mentioned in Chapter 6, technologies can give families a window into the classroom; with planning, teachers are like a tour guide at the window, pointing out things that families may not notice right away or adding information to what families already notice.

Handling Technologies as a Goal

Much the same way as young children need to learn book-handling skills, it is important for them to learn technology-handling skills (NAEYC & Fred Rogers Center 2011). Children need to be taught how to use an app, for example—teachers need to identify icons, walk children through particular steps, and perhaps remind them to not to put their finger over the camera. However, handling skills are best learned as children are using technologies rather than as the sole purpose and goal of an activity.

Tools work best when used to achieve a purpose, not in isolation. For example, if someone asks me to demonstrate how to use an app, they often quickly forget most of what I showed them and may even ask me to show them again days later. Learning how to use an app works much better when they explore the app functionalities with a little support. If they know what the app is supposed to do, they can explore functionalities, make mistakes, and delete first attempts. Now they have already started to make sense of how the app works, so any questions they ask me are connected to what they already know. The process of using the app crystalizes even more after they have used the technology to complete a project. When people have used a technology for a purpose, they can put it in context, learn from their mistakes, and be more likely to remember how to use it again.

The same holds true for children. They learn technology-handling skills through actually handling technology, not simply through demonstration. Using the GRR model discussed in Chapter 4 entails some modeling of technology use followed by supported practice, but with this model, the focus still is on using technology to accomplish a goal.

Digital Tools for Learning, Creating, and Thinking

Identifying Key Teaching Partners

Making changes to teaching practices is hard work. Finding partners to support you may be a critical part of your success. A partner can be any other professional who can offer support, such as another teacher in your program who is also making changes, an experienced teacher, a specialist, or a consultant. Consider a few questions about the kinds of partnerships that might support your goals.

Do You Need a Technology Cheerleader?

When you read the introduction to this book, did you doubt the assertion that there is no such thing as tech savviness? Did you mutter that, in fact, technology is against you or is harder for you than for others? If so, consider finding an ally who will encourage you in the hard work of trying something outside of your comfort zone. This can be another person who feels similarly about technology or someone who feels more comfortable with technology but who understands that you are not. Regardless, they must be ready to cheer on your efforts. Check in with each other for encouragement, to celebrate accomplishments, and to talk about what you've learned from your mistakes—just as you would do with the children you work with.

Do You Need a Critical Friend?

Writers and researchers sometimes use the term *critical friend* to refer to someone who will give us kind but critical feedback. This person is particularly thoughtful or perhaps also integrating technology into their program. They will make time to talk to you about your planning, reflect on projects, and help you troubleshoot. If your critical friend is also working on intentionally integrating technology in their program, this partnership can be mutually beneficial as you push and celebrate each other while working toward your goals.

Are You the Only Tech-Curious Teacher in the Classroom?

To succeed, any educational change needs the support and agreement of all teachers who are working together to implement the change. In many early childhood settings, there are coteachers or a head teacher and assistant teacher working with the children, families, and program volunteers. In some programs, not all teachers are comfortable using technology. The children are either explicitly told to go to another teacher for technology use or they figure out for themselves which teacher is more approachable with their questions. This puts an extra workload on one teacher. All teachers in the program need to be familiar with the technology available and informed of class goals for technology so that everyone can work together to achieve success.

This section has discussed possible partnerships that take place within a program, but sometimes you are the only teacher interested in studying technology integration or the only teacher at all. Organizations like NAEYC and ISTE may be places for you to connect with other teachers interested in exploring teaching with technologies in developmentally appropriate ways. NAEYC's online community platform, HELLO, offers the opportunity to join topic-focused discussion boards with early childhood professionals experts across the world. You can also find online videos, articles, and webinars at these organizations to help provide professional development opportunities for yourself or your team. (See Resources on page 103.)

Teachable Moments

One of the most powerful tools a teacher has is the teachable moment—that magical time when a child asks a question or initiates an activity that allows the teacher to build on what the child is interested in to reach learning goals. Teachable moments can seem to come out of nowhere, but it's difficult to seize a teachable moment without identifying what the child needs to know, so, in a way, teachable moments depend on planning (Clements & Wright 2022). That might seem counterintuitive; you can't plan for a child to spontaneously ask a question or initiate an activity. However, having intentional goals can help you recognize teachable moments more readily and seize them when they arise.

The moments described below were not planned for in the lesson plan, but in each example, the teacher capitalized on a moment because they had thought about using technology as a tool to achieve a particular goal.

> Miss Michelle has a goal to develop children's descriptive language. One day on the playground, the children notice a wooly caterpillar. They excitedly gather around to look at it. Miss Michelle snaps a picture so that she can build on their excitement and use technologies to work on descriptive language.
>
> Once the children are back inside, she opens up the picture. The children pinch the screen to look more closely, and Miss Michelle uses an app to record their oral observations as she asks them what they notice about their fuzzy friend. Later, she replays this recording so they can hear the vocabulary they use, and she posts it to the class's digital portfolio so they can talk about it with their families.
>
> . . . .
>
> Miss Anneliese has taught the children in her class that they can use an app to take a picture of something they have created and record talk over the picture. She wants all the children in her classroom to learn to reflect on the processes they use during play, build their oral language, and learn to communicate about their projects.
>
> Micah, a 4-year-old in her class, makes elaborate block structures; his focus is intense and he is clearly proud of his work and a little disappointed when he has to take apart the structures at cleanup time. Yet, he has refused any suggestion to use the tablet to reflect on his work.

This is on Miss Anneliese's mind when one day she notices his interest in sharing at group time. She decides to take a picture of his work at center time and invites him to record his thoughts with his peers at group time, and he agrees. He shows his picture, records a few words, and then begins talking a lot more when his classmates start asking him questions. Micah is proud and very excited to share his recorded show and talk with his family later that night.

Programs need both planned projects and teachable moments (Clements & Wright 2022). Michelle's class cooked on Thursdays, and the class would often take pictures of the steps and then record their recipe orally. Anneliese planned for story acting every week so that the children could build their storytelling and collaboration skills as they acted out the stories. In each vignette above, the teachers were intentional with their technology goals and planned specific class projects to meet their goals. Because of this planning, when teachable moments arose, the teachers could take advantage of the moment. The planning sheets in Figures 7.1 and 7.2 provide notes and examples to help you be intentional about your goals and consider how technology can support you in meeting them. (See Appendix B on page 98 for a blank planning sheet.)

Technologies are often presented to educators as something new and exciting without any real plan for integration or innovative technology use. Philanthropic organizations and celebrities have been pilloried for this approach; they fill schools with the latest technology but offer no plan, support, or explanation of how or why to use the technology. The interactive whiteboards I mentioned earlier were presented to my school as an exciting tool during a faculty meeting. There was a demonstration of how to operate the whiteboard, showing off its many features— which at the time were cutting edge—but there wasn't anything more than that. We never discussed goals, what we might need to troubleshoot, or really anything at all. As a result, many teachers tried the interactive whiteboards once and then never used them again. The teachers split into camps—those who used the whiteboards and shared their ideas and experiences, and those who lacked the confidence and curiosity to use the whiteboards and thus ignored them. Without a shared purpose, it was up to individual teachers to figure out what worked for them and the children they taught.

While teachers should be empowered to make choices about their curriculum based on the children they are working with, dividing into users and nonusers meant that we did not support the children in a systematic way that would allow all of them to learn new digital skills and meet the learning goals we all shared. New technologies still regularly show up in schools because we recognize that our lives—family, play, and work—include technologies, whether we like it or not. Teachers and school leaders must make intentional, developmentally appropriate choices about these technologies, which starts with setting goals.

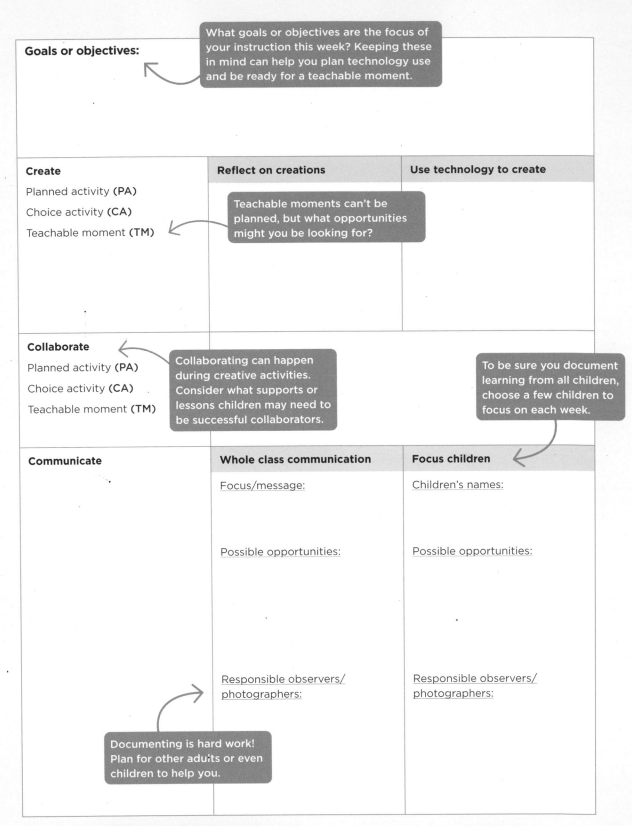

Goals or objectives:

> What goals or objectives are the focus of your instruction this week? Keeping these in mind can help you plan technology use and be ready for a teachable moment.

Create	Reflect on creations	Use technology to create
Planned activity **(PA)** Choice activity **(CA)** Teachable moment **(TM)**		
Collaborate Planned activity **(PA)** Choice activity **(CA)** Teachable moment **(TM)**		
Communicate	**Whole class communication** Focus/message: Possible opportunities: Responsible observers/ photographers:	**Focus children** Children's names: Possible opportunities: Responsible observers/ photographers:

> Teachable moments can't be planned, but what opportunities might you be looking for?

> Collaborating can happen during creative activities. Consider what supports or lessons children may need to be successful collaborators.

> To be sure you document learning from all children, choose a few children to focus on each week.

> Documenting is hard work! Plan for other adults or even children to help you.

Figure 7.1. Weekly planning sheet notes

Goals or objectives:		
1. We can learn about nature through observations. 2. We can use rich vocabulary to describe our creations. Reading to support the topic: *The Hike* by Alison Farrell and *Leaf Man* by Lois Ehlert		

Create	Reflect on creations	Use technology to create
Planned activity **(PA)** Choice activity **(CA)** Teachable moment **(TM)** (*indicates one activity in more than one category)	**PA:** Students will make leaf people. Then take picture and record a description of the natural objects in their leaf people. **TM:** Ask the kids to imagine where their leaf people might go if they traveled like the leaf man in the book.	*CA: Invite kids to make a digital puppet show with nature walk pictures as the background. **TM:** Suggest a retelling of The Hike. **TM:** Use vocabulary like observation, deciduous, and evergreen.
Collaborate Planned activity **(PA)** Choice activity **(CA)** Teachable moment **(TM)**	**PA:** Take pictures during the nature walk. Make a class book, The Nature Walk, with labels on our pictures like Alison Farrell did. *CA: Invite kids to make a digital puppet show with nature walk pictures as the background.	
Communicate	**Whole class communication**	**Focus children**
	Focus/message: Developing vocabulary from the unit. Everyone can observe! (Invite families to share pictures of nature around their homes and tell us what they observe.) Possible opportunities: Nature walk: Take pictures of deciduous and evergreen trees and share child observation photos. Outdoor play: Take pictures of kids looking at bugs and playing in the puddles. Responsible observers/ photographers: Miss Yolanda Assign child photographers for nature walk	Children's names: Asha, Daniel Possible opportunities: Asha has been making patterns with stamps in the writing center. Daniel—offer an opportunity to take a picture of his artwork and record him talking about his drawing. Responsible observers/ photographers: Miss Fatima, Mr. Andre

Figure 7.2. Sample weekly planning sheet

Next Steps

1. **Identify goals.** Use the questions and the planning sheets provided in this chapter and Appendix B to identify your goals for technologies. You might start with a goal to create, collaborate, or communicate or another goal, but plan how to intentionally use a technology to meet your goals.

2. **Identify key partners for your success.** What teachers need from a partnership will vary, so think about your needs or concerns around using technologies while teaching. Remember that partners may be people who are already on your team, but they do not have to be.

3. **Revisit your school's media policy.** Once you know what you want to do with technology, make sure the policy aligns with it. If it doesn't, talk to school administrators and families about changing the policy to make sure that you are supporting children in becoming digitally competent creators, collaborators, and communicators.

MAKING INTENTIONAL CHOICES

Where to Start

Whether you are a teacher who wants to integrate technology into your program or an administrator who is planning for technology integration for an entire school, you need to determine the program's digital culture. The learning culture of any setting includes the beliefs and actions of the administrators, teachers, children, and families. If you are aiming for a classroom community of learners, you must include all these stakeholders. Here are some questions you can ask.

What is the digital culture of your school?

New technologies are now part of cultural norms—they are imbedded in the ways in which people communicate and relate to one another. However, just as in other aspects of culture, we can expect that different groups create their own understandings and norms around technologies. How do the teachers and families in your program communicate most often? Most effectively? For example, do families respond best when teachers send papers home, call, or use email or an app? How do teachers communicate with each other? Is it only face-to-face? By phone? Do they email or text each other often? Recognizing the digital culture of your school does not dictate whether or not you integrate technologies, but it is important to consider how much of a change this will be.

What are families' current thoughts or fears about digital tools?

Your program probably already has some sort of media policy regarding the use or nonuse of images of children on the program's website or social media outlets. Families have a variety of reactions to these, which will give you information about what issues or concerns they might have about technology integration in the program.

For example, I worked in one cooperative school where families felt close to each other and were eager to share what their children did at school. This school had a relaxed media policy, with an overall permission for image use on social media or the school website; occasionally, the request for permission to use a picture was made by phone or during a face-to-face discussion with a family member. However, at a school for children who were receiving early intervention services, some of whom had profound physical or intellectual challenges, the children often rode the bus to school, so families did not have much contact with each other. In addition, many of the families were concerned about the outside world's reaction to their child or even that of families of other children in the class. This school had a clear, strict media policy. This policy needed to be rethought as the school started using technology to communicate and connect with families. Ironically, the families in this school who were most worried about their child reacted very positively to the eventual use of digital portfolios to connect them to the classroom. It was important that the teachers recognized that some families would be concerned, and talking openly with them about those concerns aided technology integration at that school.

In any community, teachers and school leaders have an ethical responsibility to have open communication with families about technology use, especially any form of digital sharing. These conversations are more fruitful if you consider the current digital culture at your school and possible concerns.

What is the comfort level of the staff?

How do the teachers in your program view themselves as users of technology? If they feel comfortable and competent with technology, you might have a discussion about setting goals for technology use. If not, acknowledge discomfort, start with a discussion of a play mindset, and talk about the acceptance of failure or mistakes before you start introducing new technology use. As a group, identify ways you can use technologies to communicate, collaborate, and create. Then discuss goals for the program, which can help teachers who are wary of technology see possible uses. Any teacher can successfully and intentionally integrate technology, but if you don't acknowledge the discomfort an educator might feel about working with new technologies, they will continue to believe that they are not good at technology and likely not pursue integrating it.

It's likely that any staff includes both teachers who feel comfortable with new technologies and those who do not. This is an opportunity for powerful partnerships. Teachers can work in teams to set goals, discuss possible projects, plan, and review together. When I started working with Debbie, she was a bit skeptical—was this just one more thing on the long list of initiatives churned out by the school board over the years? She also felt uncomfortable with technology. What helped her succeed was that I acknowledged that she would make mistakes and have failures, assured her that she would have support, and helped her see how technology could be a tool for addressing *her* teaching goals. Because of our partnership, she went from being wary of the project to co-presenting with me about developmentally appropriate technology use at a NAEYC conference.

What is the available technical support?

Troubleshooting, which is a life skill that can be applied in many settings, is a necessary part of working with technology. Anyone using technology should feel empowered to troubleshoot when they run into a problem! That said, there are times when you need to ask for help. This could mean partnering with another teacher who can help you talk through an issue, choosing apps with online support (FAQs, or customer support email/phone information) and experts to talk to, or having a designated staff member trained in instructional technology.

Depending on the complexity of the school's technology systems, some issues may go beyond general troubleshooting. Once, while I was working with a group of teachers, we could not figure out why we would sometimes get an error message when we tried to post to the class digital portfolio. We tried to problem-solve on our own, checking the Wi-Fi connection, restarting the app, and checking the FAQs on the app's website, but nothing solved our issue. After our initial troubleshooting, we turned to the school's technology officer, who figured out that the issue stemmed from the school's firewall. We couldn't solve this problem on our own; we needed outside tech support.

What resources can you tap into?

This may seem as if it should be the first question that you ask, but context matters! It is important to first consider the digital culture and context of your school and then to begin to think about the resources available to you and how you might utilize these to achieve your goals. Certainly some schools or programs have more resources than others, but remember that it's not just monetary or technological assets that will help you reach your goals. Connect with your community and consider the cultural knowledge and skills available to you. Do you have someone who is comfortable with technologies and can support those who are just beginning to use technologies? Do you know someone who is a persuasive storyteller who can help you communicate the goals of a fundraiser? Who is skilled in bargaining or requesting support and might be able to contact local businesses about partnerships? Do you have a supportive community that listens to each other and is committed to providing the best possible education for their children? This last asset may be the most important of all.

Student Sharing Checklist

Check before you add work to your portfolio:

☐ I want my family to see my work.

☐ I took a picture and it

    ☐ Is in focus

    ☐ Fits all of my work in the picture

    ☐ Doesn't have accidental fingers!

☐ I have words to explain my work.

Written words:

    ☐ I stretched my words to spell.

    ☐ I used the sight words I know.

Spoken words:

    ☐ I spoke so that others can hear me.

    ☐ I talked about this piccc of work.

    ☐ 1 included details.

Weekly Planning Sheet

Goals or objectives:		

Create Planned activity **(PA)** Choice activity **(CA)** Teachable moment **(TM)**	**Reflect on creations**	**Use technology to create**

Collaborate Planned activity **(PA)** Choice activity **(CA)** Teachable moment **(TM)**		

Communicate	**Whole class communication**	**Focus children**
	Focus/message: Possible opportunities: Responsible observers/photographers:	Children's names: Possible opportunities: Responsible observers/photographers:

From *Digital Tools for Learning, Creating, and Thinking: Developmentally Appropriate Strategies for Early Childhood Educators*, by Victoria B. Fantozzi. Copyright © 2022 by the National Association for the Education of Young Children. All rights reserved.

References

AAP (American Academy of Pediatrics). 2016. "American Academy of Pediatrics Announces New Recommendations for Children's Media Use." October 21. www.aap.org/en/news-room/news-releases/aap/2016/aap-announces-new-recommendations-for-media-use.

American Journal of Play. 2009. "The Importance of Fantasy, Fairness, and Friendship in Children's Play: An Interview with Vivian Gussin Paley." *American Journal of Play* 2 (2): 121–38.

Bales, D., K. Dalsmer, B. Blagojevic, L. Hartle, N. Chung, K. Gardner, K. Macleod, & J. Rodriguez-Vazquez. 2020. "Using Technology to Enhance Children's Learning at Home and School: Building Relationships Is Key." NAEYC (blog), September 29. www.naeyc.org/resources/blog/using-technology-enhance-childrens-learning-home-and-school.

Bers, M.U., C. González-González, & M.B. Armas-Torres. 2019. "Coding as a Playground: Promoting Positive Learning Experiences in Childhood Classrooms." *Computers & Education* 138: 130–45.

Blackwell, C. 2013. "Teacher Practices with Mobile Technology Integrating Tablet Computers into the Early Childhood Classroom." *Journal of Education Research* 7 (4): 231–55.

Bosker, B. 2016. "The Binge Breaker." *The Atlantic*. www.theatlantic.com/magazine/archive/2016/11/the-binge-breaker/501122.

Bredekamp, S., & B. Willer. 2022. "Intentional Teaching: Complex Decision Making and the Core Considerations." In *Developmentally Appropriate Practice in Early Childhood Programs Serving Children from Birth Through Age 8*, 4th ed., NAEYC, 5–23. Washington, DC: NAEYC.

Broughton, A., & M. McClary. 2020. "Creating a Culturally Responsive STEAM Curriculum." In *Each and Every Child: Teaching Preschool with an Equity Lens*, eds. S. Friedman & A. Mwenelupembe, 45–48. Washington, DC: NAEYC.

Chen, J.-Q. 2021. "Creating High-Quality STEM Experiences for All Young Learners. What Do Teachers of Young Children Need to Know?" In *Advancing Equity and Embracing Diversity in Early Childhood Education: Elevating Voices and Actions*, eds. I. Alanís & I.U. Iruka, with S. Friedman, 78–82. Washington, DC: NAEYC.

Clements, D.H., & T.S. Wright. 2022. "Teaching Content in Early Childhood Education." In *Developmentally Appropriate Practice in Early Childhood Programs Serving Children from Birth Through Age 8*, 4th ed., NAEYC, 63–79. Washington, DC: NAEYC.

Danniels, E., A. Pyle, & C. DeLuca. 2020. "The Role of Technology in Supporting Classroom Assessment in Play-Based Kindergarten." *Teaching and Teacher Education* 88. https://doi.org/10.1016/j.tate.2019.102966.

Delpit, L. 1995. *Other People's Children: Cultural Conflict in the Classroom*. New York: New Press.

Diamond, A., & K. Lee. 2011. "Interventions Shown to Aid Executive Function Development in Children 4 to 12 Years Old." *Science* 333 (6045): 959–64.

Dombrink-Green, M. 2011. "A Conversation with Vivian Gussin Paley." *Young Children* 66 (5): 90–93. https://hello.naeyc.org/HigherLogic/System/DownloadDocumentFile.ashx?DocumentFileKey=120ab5ac-0efc-481f-a589-1ffda889c08a.

Dweck, C. 2015. "Carol Dweck Revisits the Growth Mindset." *Education Week* 35 (5): 20–24.

Edwards, S., M. Henderson, D. Gronn, A. Scott, & M. Mirkhil. 2016. "Digital Disconnect or Digital Difference? A Socio-Ecological Perspective on Young Children's Technology Use in the Home and the Early Childhood Centre." *Technology, Pedagogy and Education* 26 (1): 1–17.

Falk, B. 2009. *Teaching the Way Children Learn*. New York: Teachers College Press.

Fantozzi, V.B. 2021. "'It's Everyone's iPad': Tablet Use in a Play-based Preschool Classroom." *Journal of Early Childhood Research* 19 (2): 115–27.

Fantozzi, V.B., C.P. Johnson, & A. Scherfen. 2018. "Play and Technology: An Important Intersection for Developing Literacy." *Young Children* 73 (2): 88–93.

Froebel Trust. n.d. "Froebelian Principles." Accessed November 29, 2021. www.froebel.org.uk/about-us/froebelian-principles.

Galbraith, J. 2011. "'Welcome to Our Team, Shark Boy': Making Superhero Play Visible." In *Educating Toddlers to Teachers: Learning to See and Influence the School and Peer Cultures of Classrooms*, eds. D. Fernie, S. Madrid, & R. Kantor, 37–62. New York: Hampton Press.

Gardner-Neblett, N., S.M. Curenton, & K.A. Blitch. 2017. "Viewing African American Children's Oral Language Skills as a Strength." In *African American Children in Early Childhood Education: Making the Case for Policy Investments in Families, Schools, and Communities*, eds. I.U. Iruka, S.M. Curenton, & T.R. Durden, 123–41. Bingley, UK: Emerald Publishing.

Gottschall, J. 2012. *The Storytelling Animal: How Stories Make Us Human*. Boston: Houghton Mifflin Harcourt.

Guernsey, L., M. Levine, C. Chiong, & M. Severns. n.d. P*ioneering Literacy in the Digital Wild West: Empowering Parents and Educators*. Report of the Joan Ganz Cooney Center and New America Foundation for the Campaign for Grade-Level Reading. www.joanganzcooneycenter.org/wp-content/uploads/2012/12/GLR_TechnologyGuide_final.pdf.

Harrison, E., & M. McTavish. 2018. "'i'Babies: Infants' and Toddlers' Emergent Language and Literacy in a Digital Culture of iDevices." *Journal of Early Childhood Literacy* 18 (2): 163–88. https://doi.org/10.1177/1468798416653175.

Hoffman, E.B., & K. Cipollone. 2021. "Listen to What We Hear: Developing Community Responsive Listening Centers." *Young Children* 76 (3): 6–13.

Iruka, I.U. 2022. "The Principles in Practice: Understanding Child Development and Learning in Context." In *Developmentally Appropriate Practice in Early Childhood Programs Serving Children from Birth Through Age 8*, 4th ed., NAEYC, 25–46. Washington, DC: NAEYC.

Isik-Ercan, Z. 2020. "Developing the Three Cs of Reciprocity." In *Advancing Equity and Embracing Diversity in Early Childhood Education: Elevating Voices and Actions*, eds. I. Alanís & I.U. Iruka, with S. Friedman, 61–64. Washington, DC: NAEYC.

Ladson-Billings, G. 2014. "Culturally Relevant Pedagogy 2.0: aka the Remix." *Harvard Educational Review* 84 (1): 74–84.

Levitin, D.J. 2014. *The Organized Mind: Thinking Straight in the Age of Information Overload*. New York: PLUME.

Lu, Y.-H., A.T. Ottenbreit-Leftwich, A.-C. Ding, & K. Glazewski. 2017. "Experienced iPad-Using Early Childhood Teachers: Practices in the One-to-One iPad Classroom." *Computers in the Schools: Interdisciplinary Journal of Practice, Theory, and Applied Research* 34 (1–2): 9–23.

Luby, J., & S. Kertz. 2019. "Increasing Suicide Rates in Early Adolescent Girls in the United States and the Equalization of Sex Disparity in Suicide: The Need to Investigate the Role of Social Media." *JAMA Network Open* 2 (5): e193916-e193916. https://doi.org/10.1001/jamanetworkopen.2019.3916.

Lynch, J., & T. Redpath. 2014. "'Smart' Technologies in Early years Literacy Education: A Meta-Narrative of Paradigmatic Tensions in iPad Use in an Australian Preparatory Classroom." *Journal of Early Childhood Literacy* 14 (2): 147–74.

Mancilla, L., & P. Blanco. 2022. "Engaging in Reciprocal Partnerships with Families and Fostering Community Connections." In *Developmentally Appropriate Practice in Early Childhood Programs Serving Children from Birth Through Age 8*, 4th ed., NAEYC, 145–157. Washington, DC: NAEYC.

Marsh, J. 2014. "Media, Popular Culture, and Play." In *SAGE Handbook of Play and Learning in Early Childhood*, eds. L. Brooker, M. Blaise, & S. Edwards, 403–14. London: Sage.

Marsh, J., P. Hannon, M. Lewis, & L. Ritchie. 2017. "Young Children's Initiation into Family Literacy Practices in the Digital Age." *Journal of Early Childhood Research* 15 (1): 47–60.

Masterson, M. 2022. "Planning and Implementing an Engaging Curriculum to Achieve Meaningful Goals." In *Developmentally Appropriate Practice in Early Childhood Programs Serving Children from Birth Through Age 8*, 4th ed., NAEYC, 215–251. Washington, DC: NAEYC.

McLennan, D.P. 2017. "Creating Coding Stories and Games." *Teaching Young Children* 10 (3): 18–21. www.naeyc.org/resources/pubs/tyc/feb2017/creating-coding-stories-and-games.

Mertala, P. 2017. "Wag the Dog—The Nature and Foundations of Preschool Educators' Positive ICT Pedagogical Beliefs." *Computers in Human Behavior* 69: 197–206.

Mooney, C.G. 2013. *Theories of Childhood: An Introduction to Dewey, Montessori, Erikson, Piaget, & Vygotsky*. 2nd ed. St. Paul, MN: Redleaf.

NAEYC. 2020. "Developmentally Appropriate Practice." Position statement. Washington, DC: NAEYC. www.naeyc.org/resources/position-statements/dap.

NAEYC & Fred Rogers Center for Early Learning and Children's Media. 2011. "Technology and Interactive Media as Tools in Early Childhood Programs Serving Children from Birth Through Age 8." Joint position statement. Washington, DC: NAEYC. www.naeyc.org/resources/topics/technology-and-media/resources.

NASEM (National Academies of Sciences, Engineering, and Medicine). 2018. *How People Learn II: Learners, Contexts, and Cultures*. Washington, DC: National Academies Press. https://doi.org/10.17226/24783.

Oxford English Dictionary. 1989. 2nd ed. 20 vols. Oxford: Oxford University Press. Accessed June 15, 2021. Continually updated at http://www.oed.com.

Paley, V.G. 1981. *Wally's Stories*. Cambridge, MA: Harvard University Press.

Papert, S. 1980. *Mindstorms: Children, Computers, and Powerful Ideas*. New York: Basic Books.

Papert, S., & C. Solomon. 1971. "Twenty Things to Do with a Computer." Artificial Intelligence Memo Number 248. Massachusetts Institute for Technology. https://files.eric.ed.gov/fulltext/ED077240.pdf.

Pappas, S. 2020. "What Do We Really Know About Kids and Screens?" *Monitor on Psychology* 51 (3): 42. www.apa.org/monitor/2020/04/cover-kids-screens.

Paris, D., & H.S. Alim. 2014. "What Are We Seeking to Sustain Through Culturally Sustaining Pedagogy? A Loving Critique Forward." *Harvard Educational Review* 84 (1): 85–100.

Petersen, P. 2015. "'That's How Much I Can Do!' Children's Agency in Digital Tablet Activities in a Swedish Preschool Environment." *Nordic Journal of Digital Literacy* 10 (3): 145–69.

Pew Research Center. 2021. "Internet/Broadband Fact Sheet." April 7. www.pewresearch.org/internet/fact-sheet/internet-broadband.

Prensky, M. 2001. "Digital Natives, Digital Immigrants Part 1." *On the Horizon* 9 (5): 1–6.

Resnick, M. 2017. *Lifelong Kindergarten: Cultivating Creativity Through Projects, Passion, Peers, and Play*. Cambridge, MA: MIT Press.

Rideout, V. 2017. *The Common Sense Census: Media Use by Kids Age Zero to Eight*. San Francisco, CA: Common Sense Media.

Robinson, K. 2006. "Do Schools Kill Creativity?" Filmed February 2006 in Monterey, CA. TED video, 19:01. www.ted.com/talks/sir_ken_robinson_do_schools_kill_creativity?language=en.

Rodriguez-Vazquez, J. 2020. "Access Issues." NAEYC Tech & Young Children webinar, May 18. Video, 2:51. https://www.youtube.com/watch?v=ydJ18Q2JBOY.

Sapolsky, R. 2011. "Dopamine Jackpot! Saplosky on the Science of Pleasure." YouTube video, 4:59. Excerpt of a recorded lecture at the California Academy of Sciences, February 15. Posted March 2, 2011. https://youtu.be/axrywDP9Ii0.

Sari, B., Z.K. Takacs, & A.G. Bus. 2019. "What Are We Downloading for Our Children? Best-Selling Children's Apps in Four European Countries." *Journal of Early Childhood Literacy* 19 (4): 515–32.

Scott-Little, C. With K. Reschke. 2022. "Observing, Documenting, and Assessing Children's Development and Learning." In *Developmentally Appropriate Practice in Early Childhood Programs Serving Children from Birth Through Age 8*, 4th ed., NAEYC, 159–180. Washington, DC: NAEYC.

Seiter, E. 1993. *Sold Separately: Children and Parents in Consumer Culture*. Piscataway, NJ: Rutgers University Press.

Silver, L. 2019. "Smartphone Ownership is Growing Rapidly Around the World, But Not Always Equally." Pew Research Center, February 5. www.pewresearch.org/global/2019/02/05/smartphone-ownership-is-growing-rapidly-around-the-world-but-not-always-equally.

Steiner-Adair, C., & T.H. Barker. 2013. *The Big Disconnect: Protecting Childhood and Family Relationships in the Digital Age*. New York: Harper Collins.

Straker, L., J. Zabatiero, S. Danby, K. Thorpe, & S. Edwards. 2018. "Conflicting Guidelines on Young Children's Screen Time and Use of Digital Technology Create Policy and Practice Dilemmas." *The Journal of Pediatrics* 202: 300–03. https://doi.org/10.1016/j.jpeds.2018.07.019.

Thiel, J.J. 2014. "Privileged Play: The Risky Business of Language in the Primary Classroom." *Perspectives and Provocations* 1 (1). www.earlychildhoodeducationassembly.com/privileged-play-the-risky-business-of-language-in-the-primary-classroom.html.

Twenge, J.M. 2017. "Have Smartphones Destroyed a Generation?" *The Atlantic*, September 2017. www.theatlantic.com/magazine/archive/2017/09/has-the-smartphone-destroyed-a-generation/534198.

Van Oers, B., & D. Duijkers. 2013. "Teaching in a Play-Based Curriculum: Theory, Practice and Evidence of Developmental Education for Young Children." *Journal of Curriculum Studies* 45 (4): 511–34.

Vygotsky, L. 1978. "Interaction Between Learning and Development." In *Mind in Society: The Development of Higher Psychological Processes*, eds. M. Cole, V. John-Steiner, S. Scribner, & E. Souberman, 79–92. Cambridge, MA: Harvard University Press.

Watters, A. 2015. "Education Technology and Skinner's Box." Hack Education, February 10. http://hackeducation.com/2015/02/10/skinners-box.

Webb, S., D. Massey, M. Goggans, & K. Flajole. 2019. "Thirty-Five Years of the Gradual Release of Responsibility: Scaffolding Toward Complex and Responsive Teaching." *The Reading Teacher* 73 (1): 75–83.

Wiggins, G., & J. McTighe. 2005. *The Understanding by Design*. Washington, DC: ASCD.

Wohlwend, K.E. 2011. *Playing Their Way into Literacies: Reading, Writing, and Belonging in the Early Childhood Classroom*. New York: Teachers College Press.

Wohlwend, K.E. 2017. "Who Gets to Play? Access, Popular Media and Participatory Literacies." *Early Years* 37 (1): 62–76.

Wolf, M. 2018. *Reader, Come Home: The Reading Brain in a Digital World*. New York: Harper Collins.

Zapata, A., & T.T. Laman. 2016. "'I Write to Show How Beautiful My Languages Are': Translingual Writing Instruction in English-Dominant Classrooms." *Language Arts* 93 (5): 366–78.

Zosh, J., C. Gaudreau, R.M. Golinkoff, & K. Hirsh-Pasek. 2022. "The Power of Playful Learning in the Early Childhood Setting." In *Developmentally Appropriate Practice in Early Childhood Programs Serving Children from Birth Through Age 8*, 4th ed., NAEYC, 81–107. Washington, DC: NAEYC.

Zygmunt, E., K. Cipollone, S. Tancock, J. Clausen, P. Clark, & W. Mucherah. 2018. "Loving Out Loud: Community Mentors, Teacher Candidates, and Transformational Learning Through a Pedagogy of Care and Connection." *Journal of Teacher Education* 69 (2): 127–39.

Resources

Professional Development Resources

These resources might be helpful in finding ideas or locating a source of professional development, such as a webinar or conference. All of these sources have free material or tools available, but some may have a cost associated with accessing all materials.

Common Sense Media's Education page
www.commonsense.org/education

Edutopia
www.edutopia.org/technology-integration

International Society for Technology in Education (ISTE)
www.iste.org

NAEYC Technology and Media resource page
www.naeyc.org/resources/topics/technology-and-media

NAEYC Technology and Young Children Interest Forum
www.naeyc.org/get-involved/communities/science-math-technology

HELLO
https://hello.naeyc.org/home

NAEYC's platform for early childhood educators to have conversations and create connections

Resources for Finding or Evaluating Apps

Common Sense Media App Reviews

www.commonsensemedia.org/app-reviews

Provides reviews of apps and a searchable list of apps with categories like "creative"

Kids Inclusive and Diverse Media Project (Kidmap)

www.joinkidmap.org/digchecklist

Serves many kinds of professionals in digital media; however, the DIG checklist for Inclusive, High-Quality Children's Media can be a great resource to think about the inclusivity of the digital media in your program

Index

Figures and tables are indicated by *f* and *t* respectively.

Digital Tools for Learning, Creating, and Thinking

Acknowledgments

None of this work would be possible without the wonderful teachers who welcome me into their classrooms and willingly partner with me to imagine developmentally appropriate technology uses. Thank you to Christi Johnson and Anneliese Scherfen, who invited me into their classroom when my ideas about technology use in play-based spaces were in their earliest form. Thank you to Jennifer Geskie for inviting me to partner with the teachers in her school to reimagine how they could use their digital tools. Thank you to Debbie Quintano and Michelle Posadas for learning with me and for helping me consider how technology use can support vulnerable students and families.

Thank you to my boys, Quinten and Linus. I've been watching you learn with amazement since you were born. It might not be easy to have a mom who is always watching and studying you; know that I do it with love. You continue to inspire me with your curious natures and imaginative storytelling. Thank you to my husband, Tom; you are a wonderful partner, friend, and editor. Thank you to my mom and dad for your unwavering love and belief in me. I'm sad that you will never see this book in print, but I know you are proud of me.

About the Author

Victoria B. Fantozzi, PhD, is a professor of early childhood and childhood education at Manhattanville College in Purchase, New York, where she teaches courses in emergent literacies, early childhood foundations, and research methods. Since 2015, she has partnered with schools to empower teachers to make intentional decisions about integrating technologies into their classroom practice. Her research on developmentally appropriate technologies has been published in *Young Children*, *The Reading Teacher*, and the *Journal of Early Childhood Research*, and she was a contributor to the fourth edition of *Developmentally Appropriate Practice in Early Childhood Programs Serving Children from Birth Through Age 8*. Dr. Fantozzi lives in Montclair, New Jersey, with her husband, two sons, and cat and hedgehog. This is her first book.